Growth Disorders in
CHRONIC RENAL FAILURE

O Mehls, F Schaefer and B Tönshoff

Supported by an unrestricted educational grant from Pharmacia

Professor Otto Mehls
Professor Franz Schaefer
Professor Burkhard Tönshoff
Division of Paediatric Nephrology, University Children's Hospital,
University of Heidelberg, Heidelberg, Germany

ISBN 1-903539-01-3

British Library Cataloguing-in Publication Data.

A catalogue record for this book is available from the British Library.

The publisher has made every effort to ensure that the information contained
in this publication is accurate at the time of printing. No responsibility for
loss occasioned to any person acting or refraining from acting as a result of
the material in this publication can be accepted by the authors, publisher
or sponsor.

Published by Oxford PharmaGenesis™ Ltd, 1 Tubney Warren Barns,
Tubney, Oxford OX13 5QJ, UK.

© 2003 Oxford PharmaGenesis™ Ltd

Printed and bound in the UK by Biddles Limited, England.

The opinions expressed in this publication are those of the authors and do
not necessarily reflect the opinions or recommendations of the publisher. The
dosages, indications and methods of use for the products referred to by the
authors are not necessarily the same as indicated in the package inserts for
these products and may reflect the clinical experience of the authors or may
be derived from the professional literature or other clinical sources.

The publisher can give no guarantee for information about drug dosage and
application thereof contained in this publication. In every individual case, the
respective user must check its accuracy by consulting other pharmaceutical
literature.

Foreword

Since the early 1970s, the survival of children with end-stage renal failure has been made possible by renal replacement therapy, for example long-term dialysis and renal transplantation. It soon became obvious, however, that growth failure was a major obstacle to successful rehabilitation in this patient group. For many years, growth-promoting therapy relied exclusively on dietary intervention. In the late 1980s, the introduction of recombinant human growth hormone (GH) offered an entirely new therapeutic perspective for children with uremic growth failure. GH treatment was found to improve growth rates over several years. However, concern was raised that the height gained prepubertally might be lost during the pubertal period. Reassuringly, data now available on final height indicate that the prepubertal improvement in height is maintained into adulthood.

The therapeutic success of GH stimulated extensive research on the pathophysiology of the somatotropic as well as other hormone systems in patients with uremia. It has been shown that not only are the production and metabolic clearance of hormones changed in chronic renal failure, but also that the uremic state is characterized by an insensitivity to many hormones. The molecular basis of the hormonal disturbances has been a fascinating subject of research during the past decade.

This book outlines the techniques involved in assessing growth failure in children with uremia and provides an update on the recent results of laboratory and clinical studies in the field of endocrine changes, growth failure and growth-promoting therapy.

Contents

List of abbreviations

ACTH	Adrenocorticotropic hormone
ALS	Acid-labile subunit
BI	Bioelectrical impedance
BMI	Body mass index
CAPD	Continuous ambulatory peritoneal dialysis
CCPD	Continuous cycling peritoneal dialysis
CIS	Cytokine-inducible SH2 protein
CRF	Chronic renal failure
CRH	Corticotropin-releasing hormone
CV	Coefficient of variation
$1,25(OH)_2D_3$	$1,25$-dihydroxyvitamin D_3
DHEA	Dehydroepiandrosterone
DHT	Dihydrotestosterone
EDTA	European Dialysis and Transplant Association
EPO	Erythropoietin
ESRD	End-stage renal disease
FFM	Fat-free mass
FSH	Follicle-stimulating hormone
GABA	Gamma aminobutyric acid
GFR	Glomerular filtration rate
GH	Growth hormone
GHBP	GH-binding protein
GnRH	Gonadotropin-releasing hormone
GS	Glycogen synthase
HCG	Human chorionic gonadotropin
IGF	Insulin-like growth factor
IGFBP	IGF-binding protein
JAK	Janus kinase
LH	Luteinizing hormone
PFK	Phosphofructokinase
PFM	Percentage fat mass
PTH	Parathyroid hormone
PTHrP	PTH-related peptide
RI	Resistance index
rT_3	Reverse tri-iodothyronine
SD	Standard deviation
SDS	SD score
SOCS	Suppressors of cytokine signaling
STAT	Signal transducer and activator of transcription
T_3	Tri-iodothyronine
T_4	Thyroxine
TBG	Thyroid hormone-binding globulin
TBW	Total body water
TRH	Thyrotropin-releasing hormone
TSH	Thyroid-stimulating hormone

1 Auxological techniques

Summary

Chronic renal failure (CRF) leads to growth retardation, changes in body composition and delayed puberty. As growth hormone therapy is effective in normalizing growth in children with CRF, it is important to identify growth failure at an early age. Accurate auxological measurements are therefore essential, both to assess the extent of growth retardation and to monitor the effects of treatment. This chapter describes the standard techniques for measuring longitudinal growth, body composition and the stages of puberty, and how such measurements should be interpreted in children with CRF.

1.1 Past medical history

The collection of anthropometric data from patients with renal disease should begin with a complete medical history. As well as information regarding the major milestones of the disease, the following details should also be recorded:

- prenatal history
- birth length and weight
- postnatal course of growth and development
- detailed nutritional history
- timing, duration and dosage of previous medication that could possibly interfere with growth.

Care should be taken to obtain any previous documentation of auxological measurements performed by other institutions. In addition, the height of both parents should be recorded.

1.2 Height/length measurements

Although longitudinal growth is considered one of the most important global indicators of general well-being in children, the importance of quality standards for auxological assessments is usually underestimated. Use of appropriate up-to-date standards for comparison is obviously important. Equally, technical sources of variability should be minimized. Key to high-quality measurements are the use of standardized equipment, a procedural protocol that complies with international recommendations, and the skill and experience of those making the measurements [1]. Ideally, a single observer should obtain all longitudinal measurements in an individual child. It is recommended that a series of repeated and parallel measurements should be made at regular intervals to assess and minimize intra- and interobserver variability.

The recommended procedure for measuring standing height is to place a weight on the headboard, position the child's head in the Frankfurt plane, slightly stretch the head by gentle upward pressure at the mastoid processes, and take the reading during maximal expiration. Supine length is measured in an infantometer by two observers taking care that the head is secured in the Frankfurt plane, the legs are straight, the ankles are at 90° and the footboard is in firm contact with the patient's heels. Downward pressure is exerted on the shoulders to prevent arching of the back.

1.3 Interpretation of growth data
Percentile charts

In daily clinical practice, longitudinal growth data for an individual child are assessed by comparison with reference percentiles on a growth chart. Both height distance and velocity charts are available. In height velocity charts, velocity is noted at a time-point midway between the actual measurements.

The concordance of an individual child's growth pattern with his/her genetic height potential can be judged by marking the target height on the right-hand side of the chart. The target height is obtained by the following formula.

Target height = mean parental height +6.5 cm in boys and −6.5 cm in girls

The 3rd and 97th percentiles of the target height channel correspond to 8 cm below and above the target height, respectively.

When interpreting growth patterns on such charts, it is important to recognize that longitudinal growth is not a strictly linear process. Major seasonal variation exists, and spontaneous periods of growth arrest (of up to 6 weeks) followed by 'mini-growth spurts' occur randomly in healthy children. In addition, the confounding effects of measurement errors increase exponentially

with decreasing time intervals between measurements.

Due to this inherent variability, pairs of height measurements, at least 3, better 6, and ideally 12 months apart, are required to estimate childhood growth reliably. However, even 12-month height velocity is more variable than the smoothed height velocity charts suggest; besides the pubertal growth spurt, a 'mid-childhood growth spurt', occurring around 6 years of age, and several additional oscillations of growth velocity, have been described in prepubertal children. Hence, even using 12-month measurement intervals, moderate upward or downward movement of height velocity relative to the percentiles may reflect spontaneous fluctuations, independent of disease or treatment.

In addition to the effects of physiologic growth fluctuations, analysis of the pubertal growth pattern may be influenced by treatment modalities (start of dialysis, transplantation, initiation of nasogastric or percutaneous gastric tube feeding), medication (immunosuppressive treatment after renal transplantation, treatment with GH) or by the severity of renal osteo-dystrophy (bone deformation, scoliosis). Nevertheless, analysis of the height velocity curve is a valid tool for the interpretation of pubertal changes in a uremic individual, and the analysis of synchronized growth curves is valid for group analyses in patients at different stages of CRF [2, 3] (Fig. 1).

Standard deviation score transformation

While transformation of height to a centile is perfectly acceptable and is often the easiest way to explain growth deviations to the child and family, analysis of centile charts does not lend itself to statistical

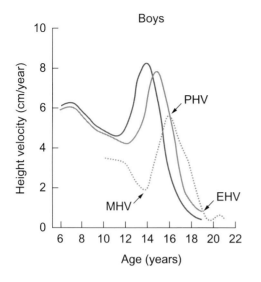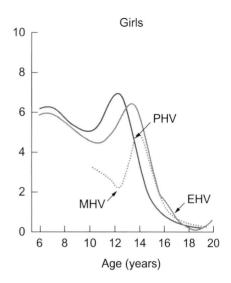

Fig. 1. *Synchronized conditional average curves of height velocity in boys and girls with average (dark lines) or late normal (pale lines) timing of puberty and in patients with end-stage renal failure (dotted lines). The definition of reference points in the growth curve, to which individual height velocity curves are aligned, permits statistical comparisons between normal and pathological growth patterns. In CRF, minimal height velocity (MHV) at pubertal onset is severely suppressed, a pubertal acceleration occurs but peak height velocity (PHV) is reduced and the duration of the growth spurt (distance from PHV to end height velocity (EHV)) is diminished.*

Adapted from [2] with permission.

analysis and is clearly of no use when the subjects are below the lowest published percentile for height. In analyzing sets of growth data, particularly in children outside the normal range, the use of standard deviation scores (SDS) is more appropriate. The SDS is calculated from the relationship:

$$SDS = x - X_i/SD_i$$

where: x is the parameter being measured. X_i is the sex- and age-specific mean and SD_i is the standard deviation (SD) of the parameter in the reference population.

The mean SDS value of the reference population is 0, and the normal range (95% confidence interval) varies between −2 and +2 SDS. SDS values are independent of age and sex, allowing comparisons of data from heterogeneous groups. SDS can be calculated for distance (i.e. height) as well as for velocity data (growth velocity).

The use of SDS to assess the stature of a child or to characterize a group of children is generally very powerful. However, several problems inherent to this normalization procedure require consideration. Commonly, a stable longitudinal course of SDS is described as 'normal growth' when the SDS is below normal. This is misleading in several ways. First, 'normal growth', after removal of the adverse circumstances that caused growth retardation, is catch-up growth (i.e. a gradual increase in SDS). Secondly, as the SD values physiologically increase over time, the absolute height deficit indicated by an SDS value is inversely related to patient age. For instance, a constant height SDS of −3 represents a height deficit of 8 cm at age 1, but almost 20 cm at age 10 years. The opposite is true for height velocity SDS; the same SDS value reflects a greater absolute deficit in growth rate in a young infant than in a late-prepubertal child. In children with CRF treated with GH, the change in height SDS in response to therapy is inversely correlated with age, whereas the change in height velocity SDS correlates positively with age. However, the absolute height velocity induced by GH treatment is age independent (Fig. 2). As the final height

deficit (in cm) and its correction are the primary outcome variables relevant to patients, treatment success may be better judged from the gain in absolute height than from relative changes in height SDS.

Another problem is the interpretation of SDS data in the peripubertal age range. Patients with a late onset of puberty (such as children with CRF) grow at a low prepubertal rate at a time when their healthy peers are already experiencing their pubertal growth acceleration. Hence, any comparison of a child with developmental delay to age-matched reference groups will introduce a major bias in SDS calculation. This problem is relevant for height SDS and much more so for height velocity SDS, which will appear excessively low before the child enters puberty and excessively high during the pubertal growth spurt, occurring at a time when the average child has almost

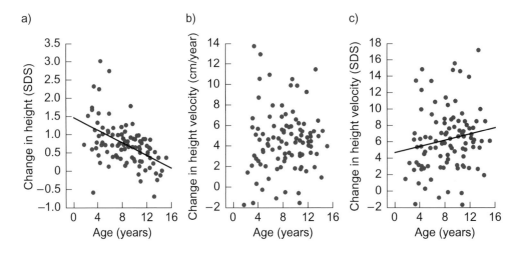

Fig. 2. Change in (a) height SDS, (b) height velocity and (c) height velocity SDS during the first year of GH treatment as a function of age. While the absolute height velocity increment induced by treatment is independent of age, a positive correlation with age appears when the change in height velocity is standardized, and there is a negative correlation when the change in height SDS is related to age.

From [4] with permission.

stopped growing. It has been proposed that height and height velocity should be related to bone age rather than chronological age. This may be acceptable in simple pubertal delay but usually not in chronic illnesses, such as CRF, and particularly in glucocorticoid-treated patients, where osseous differentiation is frequently dissociated from the maturational state of a child. A better approach is to use extrapolated prepubertal height velocity standards to compare late-prepubertal growth rates in late-maturing children [5].

1.4 Maturity indicators

In the peripubertal stage of growth and development, the phenotypical stages of puberty provide a convenient and reliable assessment of maturation. The staging system of Tanner has been universally accepted [6, 7]. As the onset and progression of pubertal development has critical implications for growth and psychological adjustment, Tanner staging should be performed at least every 3 months in peripubertal children with CRF.

Breast stages for girls

Stage 1: Pre-adolescent: elevation of papilla only.
Stage 2: Breast-bud stage: elevation of breast and papilla as a small mound; enlargement of areolar diameter.
Stage 3: Further enlargement and elevation of breast and areola with no separation of their contours.
Stage 4: Projection of areola and papilla to form a secondary mound above the level of the breast.
Stage 5: Mature stage: projection of papilla only, a result of recession of the areola to the general contour of the breast.

Genitalia stages for boys

Stage 1: Pre-adolescent: testes, scrotum and penis are about the same size and proportion as in early childhood.
Stage 2: Enlargement of scrotum and testes. The skin of the scrotum reddens and changes in texture, with little or no enlargement of the penis at this stage.
Stage 3: Enlargement of the penis, which occurs at first mainly in length, and further growth of testes and scrotum.
Stage 4: Increased size of the penis with growth in breadth, development of glans, and further enlargement of testes and scrotum with increasing darkening of scrotal skin.
Stage 5: Genitalia are adult in size and shape.

Pubic hair stages for both sexes

Stage 1: Pre-adolescent: the vellus over the pubis is not further developed than on the abdominal wall.
Stage 2: Sparse growth of long, slightly pigmented downy hair, straight or only slightly curled, appearing chiefly at the base of the penis or along the labia.
Stage 3: Considerably darker, coarser, and more curled. The hair spreads sparsely over the junction of the pubis.
Stage 4: Hair now resembles adult type, but the area covered is still considerably smaller than in the adult, with no spread to the medial surface of the thighs.
Stage 5: Adult in quantity and type, with distribution of the horizontal pattern. Spread to the medial surface of the thighs but not up linea alba or elsewhere above the base of the inverse triangle.

As the Tanner stages (particularly genitalia [G] stages) are relatively subjective, orchidometry was introduced by Prader as a more objective means to stage pubertal progress in boys. Testicular volume is easily assessed by comparison with standard ovoids (the Prader orchidometer). Reference data are available [8].

Some caveats must be made in applying these criteria in children with chronic renal disease. Dysplastic kidney disorders frequently involve not only the kidneys but also the urogenital tract. Patients may present with genito-urinary anomalies (cryptorchidism, hypospadias, epispadias, micropenis, labial fusion, etc.), which may render the application of Tanner staging or orchidometry extremely difficult. Endocrine abnormalities associated with uremia and/or the use of various drugs for the treatment of renal failure may cause abnormalities of primary and secondary sexual characteristics. For example, patients with CRF may be hyperprolactinemic and may develop gynecomastia independently of puberty. In transplanted patients, cyclosporine A-induced hypertrichosis may confound pubic hair staging.

1.5 Body composition

Children with CRF are at risk of various acute and chronic alterations in body composition. In infancy, uremic anorexia leads to malnutrition and wasting. This can be prevented or corrected by tube feeding; however, monitoring of nutritional status by weight alone is difficult due to fluid imbalances resulting from renal salt and water loss or, in advanced renal failure, from insufficient fluid elimination. Also, while infants on forced feeding regimens tend to become obese, it is usually unclear whether normalization of lean body mass is achieved.

In children on dialysis, wasting of fat-free mass (FFM) is frequently masked by occult water retention. Estimation of 'dry weight' in a constantly growing child is one of the most difficult challenges to the pediatric nephrologist.

After renal transplantation, glucocorticoid treatment causes a variable Cushingoid appearance. In the absence of routine tools to assess body composition, it is often difficult to differentiate changes in body fat from changes in metabolically active fat-free tissue.

Several tools are available to assess body composition in these settings. The following text outlines inexpensive and non-invasive methodologies that can be used outside an auxological research setting.

Body mass index

Body mass index (BMI) – body weight (in kg) divided by the square of height (in meters) – has gained wide acceptance as a marker of obesity in adults. The rationale for using BMI over a simple weight-to-height ratio lies in the assumption that FFM is directly proportional to the square of height, and that the weight at a given height-squared should be a linear function of the relative fat mass of an individual. BMI is strongly age dependent, necessitating standardization of the index according to the age of the child.

Normalization to conventional SDS (as described above) produces biased results, as the distribution of body weight and BMI is not Gaussian but markedly skewed towards the upper range. Recently, a simple technique was proposed to standardize skewed data by calculating a skewness factor (L), in addition to the median (M) and variance (S), for reference distributions [9]. Interpolation of reference L, M and S values at a given age allows normally distributed SDS values for any parameter with a skewed distribution to be calculated using the following formula:

$$SDS = [(Y/M(t))^{L(t)} - 1] / (L(t)*S(t))$$

where: Y is the measured individual value of the parameter of interest and t is the interpolated independent variable (usually age).

BMI reference data processed for application of the LMS method are available for pediatric populations in several European countries (see for example [10]; Fig. 3), and can be used for cross-sectional and longitudinal analyses of body composition in children. The LMS normalization procedure for BMI is particularly helpful in young infants, where absolute weight or raw BMI data are not suitable for even short-term monitoring of the nutritional state due to highly dynamic spontaneous changes with age. Rapid normalization of BMI SDS by tube feeding has been observed in 25 young infants with end-stage renal disease (ESRD) [12].

Due to the highly dynamic changes of BMI during childhood, the use of chronological age to standardize BMI data is questionable in patients with growth disorders. The body composition of a growth-retarded child should be in concordance with height age rather than with chronological age. As an illustration of this problem, a group of pediatric renal allograft recipients with a mean height SDS of −2 showed apparently normal BMI SDS (0.1 ± 1.2) when related to chronological age, despite a typical moderately Cushingoid appearance. When standardized to height age, a more appropriate mean BMI SDS of 1 ± 1.2 was obtained (Fig. 4).

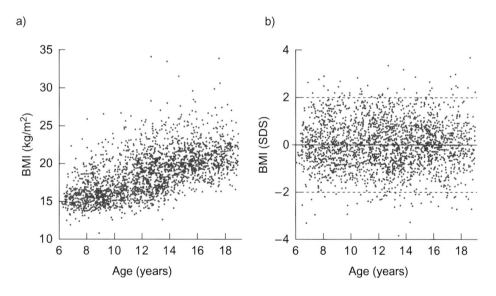

a)   b)

Fig. 3. *Transformation of (a) skewed BMI data to (b) normally distributed SDS by the LMS method (see text) in 2554 healthy schoolchildren and adolescents aged 6–19 years. The L, M and S reference values derived from and reapplied in this population were published in [10].*

From [11] with permission.

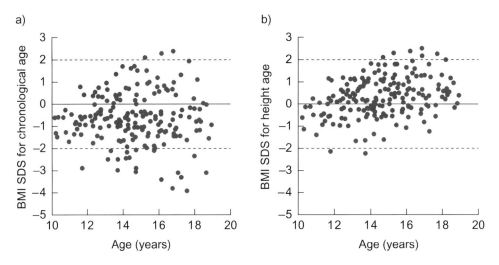

Fig.4. Effect of BMI normalization for (a) chronological versus (b) height age in peripubertal renal allograft recipients. Growth retardation erroneously suggests normal or even reduced BMI SDS despite Cushingoid appearance when referring to chronological age. Correction for growth retardation by normalization to height age reveals mild obesity in this population.

From [11] with permission.

Skinfold thickness and percentage fat mass

Although BMI is a reasonable predictor of cardiovascular risk in obese individuals, it has been shown to be a very crude measure of body fat stores [10]. These should be estimated whenever possible by a more direct assessment. Skinfold thickness measurements remain the most widely available tool to quantify body fat stores. Skinfold thicknesses are usually assessed using specifically designed calipers (e.g. the Harpenden skinfold caliper) at four reference sites: the biceps and triceps skinfolds determined midway between the acromion and olecranon processes at the anterior and posterior surface of the right arm, the subscapular skinfold 1 cm caudally and medially to the right scapular angle, and the suprailiac skinfold thickness 1 cm above the superior anterior rim of the right iliac crest. The thickness reading depends on the angle at which the caliper is placed, the texture and hydration of the skin and subcutaneous tissue, and the duration of the pressure exerted by the caliper arms. Therefore, the reproducibility of single skinfold measurements is poor, with typical intra- and interobserver coefficients of variation (CV) of 3–7% and 8–20%, respectively [13].

Despite the limited precision of a single skinfold thickness assessment, acceptable reproducibility can be achieved when multi-site skinfold measurements are integrated in estimates of whole-body percentage fat mass (PFM) [13]. Slaughter and co-workers developed and validated a set of sex- and age-specific PFM prediction equations based on a multicomponent model of body composition allowing for the variable FFM density in childhood [14] (Table 1).

Table 1. Sex- and age-specific percentage fat mass (PFM) prediction equations.

Boys:
If subscapular + triceps skinfold thickness ≤ 35 mm and Tanner G-stage ≤ 2:
PFM = 1.21 × (subscapular + triceps) − 0.008 × (subscapular + triceps)^2 − 1.7

If subscapular + triceps skinfold thickness ≤ 35 mm and Tanner G-stage = 3:
PFM = 1.21 × (subscapular + triceps) − 0.008 × (subscapular + triceps)^2 − 3.4

If subscapular + triceps skinfold thickness ≤ 35 mm and Tanner G-stage ≥ 4:
PFM = 1.21 × (subscapular + triceps) − 0.008 × (subscapular + triceps)^2 − 5.5

If subscapular + triceps skinfold thickness > 35 mm:
PFM = 0.783 × (subscapular + triceps) + 1.6

Girls:
If subscapular + triceps skinfold thickness ≤ 35 mm:
PFM = 1.33 × (subscapular + triceps) − 0.013 × (subscapular + triceps)^2 − 2.5

If subscapular + triceps skinfold thickness > 35 mm:
PFM = 0.546 × (subscapular + triceps) + 9.7

From Slaughter et al. *Skinfold equations for estimation of body fatness in children and youth.* Hum Biol *1988;60:709–23 with permission.*

Moderately experienced caliper users should be able to achieve fat mass estimates with an intra-observer CV of less than 2%, corresponding to 0.4% of fractional fat mass [13]. Pediatric reference data for PFM based on the Slaughter equations are available [10] (Fig. 5). These tables contain L, M and S reference values, which allow the calculation of SDS values for parametric statistical analyses of the markedly skewed PFM (see page 6).

Bioelectrical impedance analysis
Bioelectrical impedance (BI) is the conductive resistance of a biological tissue exposed to an alternating electrical current. As only electrolyte-containing fluids, but not adipocytes, conduct electrical currents, whole-body BI is inversely related to the total body water (TBW) content. BI is measured by attaching two pairs of modified ECG electrodes to the right wrist and ankle, applying a current through the outer electrodes and measuring the voltage loss between the inner two electrodes. The measured impedance value can be transformed to a 'resistance index' (RI = height^2/impedance) in order to normalize for the length and volume of the measured subject. The RI displays a close linear relationship with TBW. Because TBW is a constant fraction of the FFM in normally hydrated subjects, the RI can be used to estimate both TBW and FFM [13, 15]. The high technical precision, non-invasiveness and low cost of the method, together with its minimal requirement for observer experience and patient cooperation, make it a very attractive tool for the routine assessment of the state of hydration and fat/FFM

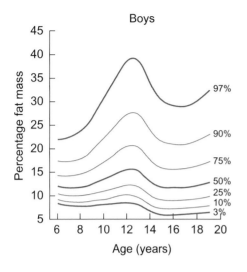
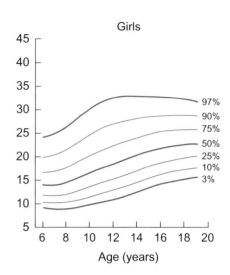

Fig. 5. *Reference values for skinfold-derived percentage fat mass estimates in boys and girls aged 6–19 years.*

Adapted from [11] with permission.

distribution in clinical practice. BI is particularly useful in children with CRF, where it is important to have a precise estimate of dry weight.

However, several potential problems connected with the interpretation of BI measurements require consideration. First, the electrolyte content of fat-free fluids changes with age during childhood, necessitating the use of specific TBW and FFM prediction equations for children [16]. Secondly, the hydration of fat-free tissue, as well as the size of the interstitial fluid compartment, may be altered in a disease-specific manner [17]. Therefore, estimations of TBW and FFM from BI in children on dialysis or after renal transplantation may only be valid using prediction equations developed for these particular populations. Thirdly, children with CRF may exhibit marked alterations and variability of their TBW content. While TBW itself may be

measured correctly by use of appropriate prediction equations, the large individual variability of the TBW–FFM relationship renders FFM prediction extremely problematic in this patient group.

In healthy children and adolescents aged between 5 and 18 years, FFM can be predicted from BI by the following equation, with a residual error of 5.8% [13].

$$\text{FFM [kg]} = 0.65 \times (\text{height}^2/\text{impedance}) \text{ [cm}^2/\text{Ohm]} + 0.68 \times \text{age [years]} + 0.15$$

The following specific prediction equation for TBW in children on hemo- or peritoneal dialysis has also been developed and cross-validated [18, 19].

$$\text{TBW [l]} = 0.144 \times (\text{height}^2/\text{impedance}) \text{ [cm}^2/\text{Ohm]} + 0.40 \times \text{weight [kg]} + 1.99$$

Notably, BI measurements are almost completely unaffected by the presence of dialysis fluid in the abdomen [20]. Resistance is mainly determined by the hydration of the arm and leg where the electrodes are placed. Due to this phenomenon, drainage of the peritoneal dialysis fluid is not required prior to assessment in daily practice.

The regular (i.e. monthly) documentation of BI values is a simple, useful adjunct to clinical assessment and blood pressure recording in the interpretation of weight changes in an individual. Impedance values are rather stable over time, and any increase in body weight associated with a decrease of BI values may indicate increasing fluid retention. In contrast, weight gain in the presence of stable or rising impedance values indicates an increases in body solids. A pediatric reference chart for BI is shown in Fig. 6.

BI can also be used to assess FFM in renal allograft recipients, in whom hydration is usually stable but gluco-corticoid-induced Cushingoid changes of body composition occur that may be due to changes in lean body mass, fat mass or both. The low cost, non-invasive nature and wide availability of BI make it a useful technique in the clinical assessment of changes in body composition after renal transplantation. In 15 patients studied longitudinally during the first year after transplantation, weight gain beyond the third post-transplant month was found to be due not only to increasing fat deposition, but also to an increase in FFM [21].

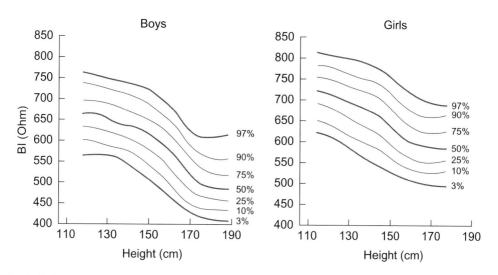

Fig. 6. *Reference percentiles for bioelectrical impedance (BI) values relative to height, derived from 1276 boys and 1278 girls.*

Adapted from [11] with permission.

2 Clinical presentation: growth and developmental disorders

Summary

Chronic renal failure (CRF) affects growth and development differently during infancy, mid-childhood and puberty. Growth disturbances during early infancy are common in children with CRF, and, if left untreated during this period, may result in severe growth retardation. During mid-childhood, growth largely parallels that seen in normal children, although there is some variability, which appears to be related to the degree of renal dysfunction. Onset of puberty and development of secondary sexual characteristics are usually delayed in adolescents with CRF, including those who have undergone renal transplantation and those on dialysis. Once started, however, puberty generally proceeds at a normal rate, although reproductive function may be permanently impaired in both sexes. However, the duration of the pubertal growth spurt is shortened.

Dialysis appears to have a beneficial effect on bone maturation, which is otherwise invariably retarded in those with long-standing renal failure. Final height is typically compromised in CRF, with approximately 50% of patients achieving adult heights below the third percentile. There is thus a clear role for growth hormone therapy in treating the severe growth failure that may occur in patients with congenital or acquired renal disorders.

2.1 Impact of developmental stage

The regulatory mechanisms of statural growth during childhood differ in the successive stages of development. During the first 2 years of life, growth is mainly driven by nutritional factors, particularly the intake of energy and protein. In later childhood, growth appears to depend mainly on the somatotropic axis, with nutrition exerting a more permissive influence. During puberty, the growth process is dominated by the gonadotropic hormone axis, which stimulates and finally terminates body growth by a direct action on the growth cartilage and by modulation of the somatotropic axis. In view of these differences in growth regulation, growth in renal disorders will be described separately for the periods of infancy, mid-childhood and puberty.

The first 2 years of life are the most dynamic period of growth. Some 30% of total postnatal statural growth is normally achieved during this period. Any disturbance of growth in infancy has a greater impact on growth potential than at later stages of development. Spontaneous growth in children with congenital CRF is characterized by a rapidly increasing height deficit during the first 2 years of life. Thereafter, the growth pattern parallels the normal growth channel observed in mid-childhood. In the late prepubertal period, height velocity again decreases disproportionately, resulting in a further deviation from the normal percentiles. A later pubertal growth spurt of diminished amplitude eventually results in an irreversible loss of growth potential, leading to a stunted adult height.

Infancy

Untreated CRF during early infancy is usually associated with severe growth retardation [22–26]. The loss in relative height is greatest during the first year of life, particularly during the first 6 months. A detailed analysis of the early infantile growth pattern according to the Infancy–Childhood–Puberty model of Karlberg *et al.* revealed that the infancy growth phase, starting in intrauterine life and ending during the second year of life, is affected in 50% of patients with CRF [27]. Height SDS was already slightly reduced at birth, decreased further during the first 3 post-natal months, stabilized between 3 and 9 months and decreased again between 10 and 12 months of life. After a transient stabilization of growth rate, a further loss in relative height apparently occurred between 0.75 and 1.5 years of age. In the mechanistic Infancy–Childhood–Puberty model [27], this period reflects the transition from the infancy to the childhood growth phase (Fig. 7). The height deficit acquired during this period may be due either to a delayed onset of the childhood growth phase or to a

temporary 'offset' of the childhood growth phase. In unselected patients studied by Karlberg and co-workers [27], a loss of height SDS of nearly 4 SD was observed at the end of the third year of life. The reasons for this secondary deterioration of growth in infancy, which may occur despite adequate nutritional and medical supplementation, are still poorly understood. If the hypothesis that the childhood growth component is mainly driven by the somatotropic axis is correct, the growth patterns during this transitional period could represent changes between periods of normal (infancy and childhood components operative) and impaired GH action (only infancy component intact). With regard to early postnatal life, anorexia, water and electrolyte imbalances caused by uremia, recurrent vomiting, catabolic responses to infections, and metabolic acidosis have been cited as the main factors compromising this period of growth.

Mid-childhood

During the mid-childhood period, growth is mainly regulated by endocrine mechanisms. Patients with a reduced renal mass, for example those with hypoplastic renal disease, usually grow along the percentile attained at the end of infancy [28]. Patients who develop CRF after the second year of life lose relative height early in the course of the disease and follow the growth percentile after stabilization of the disease process. The degree of renal dysfunction is the principal determinant of the variability in growth during this period. A retrospective analysis in patients with hypoplastic kidney disorders showed a slightly but continuously lower annual growth rate in patients with a glomerular filtration rate (GFR) below 25 ml/min/1.73 m^2 compared

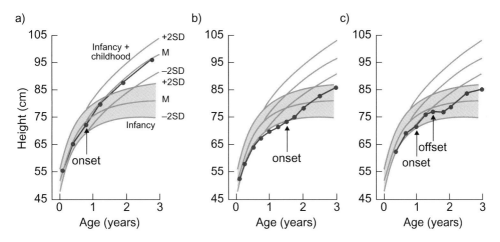

Fig. 7. Examples of normal and abnormal growth patterns observed in CRF. (a) The normal growth pattern in a patient with CRF, characterized by a smooth decelerating path during the infancy phase and a smooth transition into the infancy + childhood phase at about 0.75 years of age, representing the age at onset of the childhood component. (b) The growth curve for a CRF patient with a normal smooth path of growth in infancy, but with delayed childhood onset (> 1 year of age), seen in 36% of all children with congential CRF. (c) CRF patient with onset of the childhood component of growth at 1 year of age followed by a childhood offset period (i.e. a growth curve returning back to the infancy growth pattern seen in 60% of the patients). The reference values for infancy (grey) and infancy + childhood (open) show means (M) ± 2 SD.
Adapted from [27] with permission.

with patients above this limit, cumulating in a mean height difference of 6 cm between these subgroups at the age of 10 years [28] (Fig. 8). Growth rates were consistently correlated with the patients' average GFR, although only 10–15% of the variability in growth was actually accounted for by this parameter. The degree of anemia, metabolic acidosis and malnutrition contributed only marginally to the annual growth rate. It is suggested that catch-up growth is continuously suppressed in the uremic milieu. The percentile-parallel growth pattern during the mid-childhood period may therefore reflect a net balance between the growth-suppressive effect of uremia and the inherent tendency for catch-up growth.

Puberty

The onset of puberty is usually delayed in adolescents with CRF. Roughly, two-thirds of adolescents with ESRD enter puberty beyond the normal age range [29]. The early cross-sectional survey published by the European Dialysis and Transplant Association (EDTA) Registry showed that sexual maturation was generally retarded in adolescent boys and girls with ESRD [30, 31]. In all, 50% of children achieved the subsequent pubertal stages beyond the age when 97% of a normal population have passed these maturation hallmarks [31, 32]. Later reports confirmed this degree of pubertal delay [30, 33]. Late puberty was observed both in children on dialysis and after renal transplantation.

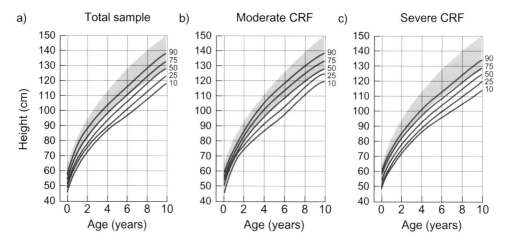

Fig. 8. *Mixed-longitudinal percentile curves (10th–90th) of height for (a) total patient sample, (b) patients with moderate CRF (GFR during the observation period > 25 ml/min/1.73 m²), and (c) patients with severe CRF (mean GFR < 25 ml/min/1.73 m²). The shaded area represents the 3rd–97th percentile of height in healthy boys.*

Adapted from [28] with permission.

More recently, the Cooperative Study Group for Pubertal Development in CRF followed some 70 patients prospectively through the process of pubertal maturation. In this study the onset of puberty was delayed by an average of 2–2.5 years [2]. The start of genital maturation (Tanner G2) was delayed by 1.8 years in uremic and 2.5 years in transplanted boys. Full genital maturation was achieved with a delay of 2.2 and 3.2 years, respectively. Thus, once started, puberty appears to proceed at a normal rate. However, in individual patients, particularly in those on long-term dialysis, pubertal maturation may be arrested for years.

The age at attainment of pubic hair stage 2 was delayed by 1.3 years in uremic and 1.5 years in transplanted boys [2] compared with healthy controls [34]. At attainment of adult pubic hair phenotype, the uremic boys were 1.9 years and the transplanted boys 3.5 years older than the healthy controls.

The transplanted boys were the most retarded, despite cyclosporine A-induced hypertrichosis, which may lead to an erroneously early pubic hair staging. According to the EDTA Registry, almost half of the girls treated by dialysis or renal transplantation failed to menstruate before the upper normal age limit of 15 years. Menarche tended to occur later in transplanted than in dialyzed girls [31].

Unlike the development of secondary sexual characteristics, which is delayed but not permanently halted in uremia, reproductive function may be permanently impaired. In autopsy studies in boys with CRF, germ-cell depletion in the testicular tubules has been described [35]. These changes seem not to be reversible by renal transplantation [36]. Persistently reduced sperm counts were observed in 10 of 12 successfully transplanted young adults who had suffered from ESRD during childhood [36]. Erectile dysfunction and decreased libido and fertility are primarily organic in nature and are due to uremia as well as to other comorbid conditions, fatigue and psychosocial factors [37].

The frequency of conception is decreased in women with CRF, and pregnancy is very uncommon in adolescents with ESRD. If pregnancy occurs, however, major changes in clinical management, such as prolonged dialysis sessions, are required. The percentage of surviving infants ranges from 70% to 100% in women with CRF on conservative treatment or after renal transplantation [36] and from 50% to 80% in women on dialysis [38–40]. Intrauterine growth retardation is frequent, and birth weight is reduced by nearly 1 kg [33, 37, 38].

The height gain achieved during the pubertal growth spurt is usually reduced [2, 41–44]. In a longitudinal analysis of the growth curves of 29 adolescents with various degrees of CRF, the growth spurt started with an average delay of 2.5 years [2]. The degree of the delay was correlated with the duration of CRF. Although a distinct acceleration of growth during puberty occurred, the total pubertal height gain was reduced in both sexes to approximately 50% of normal late-maturing children. This reduction was due to a marked suppression of the late pre-spurt height velocity, a subnormal peak height velocity and a shortening of the pubertal growth period by 1 year in boys and 1.5 years in girls (see Fig. 1). Notably, the prolonged prepubertal growth phase, resulting from the delayed onset of the pubertal growth spurt, permitted the patients to grow to an almost normal immediate pre-spurt height (−1 SDS in boys, +0.1 SDS in girls). Subsequently, relative height was gradually lost during the pubertal growth spurt, resulting in an average relative height of −2.9 SDS in boys and −2.3 SDS in girls.

In prepubertal children with long-standing renal failure, bone maturation is invariably retarded [30, 45–47]. In dialysis patients, skeletal maturation is increasingly retarded before the start of puberty and then accelerates dramatically. This observation and the fact that uremic boys respond to exogenous application of testosterone esters by an exaggerated increase in skeletal maturation [47] suggests that the sensitivity of the growth plate to sex steroids is at least conserved. Because proliferation (i.e. growth) cannot keep pace with differentiation (i.e. bone maturation), growth potential may be irreversibly lost during puberty in uremia.

In contrast, in many transplant patients, an apparent standstill of bone maturation is observed, even when the patient is growing and puberty is progressing. This phenomenon is thought to be related to direct interference of corticosteroids with the differentiation of the growth plate. Despite the delayed bone age, late growth is usually not observed [2, 48, 49]. In fact, the successive stages of the pubertal growth spurt seem to occur at increasingly earlier bone ages than would be assumed in a normal population [2].

2.2 Final height

A crucial question in the rehabilitation of children with chronic renal disease is the degree to which final height is compromised. Of the patients with childhood-onset ESRD in the EDTA Registry, 50% achieved adult heights below the 3rd percentile. Children who continued dialysis until adulthood reached a lower mean final height than children who received a renal transplant [48, 50–55]. Final height appeared to be more severely compromised in boys than in girls. However, this reflects mainly the higher incidence of congenital nephropathies in boys. Final height is most compromised in patients with severe congenital renal disorders, among which nephropathic cystinosis leads to the most obvious growth retardation [56]. However, patients with acquired glomerular diseases usually exhibit a very marked loss in height SDS in the early course of the disease, resulting in the need for growth-promoting treatment in a large proportion of this patient group.

3 Etiology of growth failure in chronic renal failure

Summary

Growth retardation in chronic renal failure (CRF) appears to be caused by a combination of factors. From an early age, CRF is accompanied by a loss of appetite. This is particularly important in light of the strong association between malnutrition and growth retardation during infancy. Ensuring adequate calorie intake may help growth. Additionally, a progressive loss of water and/or electrolytes, as seen in congenital renal diseases, is associated with other growth disorders. Impaired excretion of ammonia due to kidney dysfunction causes metabolic acidosis. This, in turn, has profound effects on the regulation of growth hormone (GH) and insulin-like growth factor I, and may contribute to GH insensitivity. The extent to which the progressive development of anemia in children with CRF contributes to growth impairment is unknown; however, this condition may be treated using recombinant erythropoietin. Renal osteodystrophy can result in gross skeletal deformities, which may contribute to growth retardation. Once renal osteodystrophy has developed, treatment of the associated disturbances in vitamin D and parathyroid hormone does not appear to improve growth. Although, in principle, transplantation restores the conditions for normal growth, this is not always the case. The administration of corticosteroids or the presence of a poorly functioning graft both have growth-suppressive effects.

The pathogenesis of impaired growth in CRF is complex and only partially understood. Although a particular cause can occasionally be found, a combination of several factors is generally responsible for growth impairment (Table 2). Furthermore, the patient's age, the type, duration and severity of renal disease, the treatment modality and the patient's social environment all play important roles.

3.1 Protein-calorie malnutrition

One of the cardinal abnormalities associated with CRF is a loss of appetite. Spontaneous food intake is usually low when related to the patient's age, but normal when adjusted for body mass [57, 58]. Thus, it is difficult to know whether low energy intake is the cause or the consequence of impaired growth in children. The same is true for the body protein content of children with CRF and

Table 2. Etiology of growth impairment in CRF.

- Genetic factors
  - parental height
  - gender
  - syndromal disorder (with kidney disorder as a part)
- Age at start of CRF
- Duration of CRF
- Residual renal function
- Treatment modalities for CRF
- Energy malnutrition
- Water and electrolyte disturbances
- Metabolic acidosis
- Hormonal disorders
  - disturbance of parathyroid hormone and vitamin D (renal osteodystrophy)
  - disturbance of the somatotropic hormonal axis
  - disturbance of the gonadotropic hormonal axis
  - disturbance of insulin/glucose metabolism
  - disturbance of other hormones

short stature, which is adequate for height but not for age [59]. It is still not clear whether uremia leads to a reduction in anabolism or to an increase in catabolism. Animal studies support both mechanisms, whereas studies in humans suggest increased catabolism as the main alteration of tissue metabolism. At any given level of protein intake, the conversion of dietary to body protein is less efficient in uremic compared with pair-fed control animals [60]. Impaired protein synthesis, resistance to the anabolic effects of insulin and increased muscle breakdown may all contribute to poor growth. Adequate energy intake is required for anabolism and growth. Energy intake is correlated with growth rate if it is less than 80% of the recommended dietary allowance [61]. However, augmentation of energy intake above this level results in obesity rather than in a further stimulation of growth [61, 62]. Energy malnutrition is particularly prevalent in uremic infants during the first year of life (see Chapter 2, page 14; *Infancy*), when the metabolic rate in relation to body mass is high. Height SDS is correlated with body cell mass and serum transferrin or albumin, emphasizing the importance of malnutrition for growth failure in this age group [22, 63, 64]. In contrast to deficient calorie intake, protein malnutrition is infrequently seen in children with CRF [57, 58]. In a prospective study in which protein intake was limited to the safe levels recommended by the World Health Organization (i.e. 0.8–1.1 g/kg/day) but ensuring adequate calorie intake, no impairment of weight gain and length gain was seen over 3 years [65].

3.2 Disturbances of water and electrolyte metabolism

Many congenital renal diseases that slowly progress towards CRF lead to a loss of electrolytes and a reduced ability of the kidney to concentrate urine. In particular, sodium chloride is lost in patients with obstructive uropathies and renal hypoplasia, and potassium is lost in patients with tubular damage, particularly in nephropathic cystinosis. Polyuria, an expression of the reduced ability of the kidney to concentrate urine, is seen mainly in patients with Fanconi's syndrome and in nephronophthisis.

It is not possible to assess independently the extent to which disturbances in water and electrolyte metabolism contribute to growth retardation in individual patients with CRF. The probability of these factors being significant has, however, been shown by analogous clinical and animal studies. In rats, sodium deficiency decreases protein synthesis and growth, which is only partially reversible by sodium repletion [66, 67]. Recently, evidence has been provided that some of the effects previously attributed to sodium deficiency were actually caused by concomitant depletion of chloride. Selectively removing chloride from a sodium-repleted diet caused growth retardation and diminished muscle protein synthesis [68]. In children with Bartter's syndrome, sodium, chloride and potassium deficits are accepted causes of growth disorders. The same applies both to patients with familial chloride diarrhea and to infants with a reduced chloride diet [69].

3.3 Metabolic acidosis

Metabolic acidosis is almost inevitably observed in CRF if there is a 50% reduction in normal GFR. This acidosis is primarily due to the kidney's reduced ability to excrete ammonia. The severity of the acidosis is aggravated by nutritional protein and acid load, catabolism and altered electrolyte balance. Metabolic acidosis in uremic rats is associated with increased glucocorticoid production and increased protein degradation by activating branched-chain ketoacid catabolism and the ubiquitin-proteasome pathway [70–74]. However, these consequences are mainly based on short-term observations, and long-term adaption of the acidotic organism is not well studied. Moreover, metabolic acidosis has profound effects on the somatotropic hormone axis, down-regulating spontaneous GH secretion [75], the expression of GH receptor and insulin-like growth factor I (IGF-I) mRNA [76] and both baseline and GH-stimulated serum IGF-I concentrations [77]. Thus, metabolic acidosis *per se* seems to result in a state of GH insensitivity.

3.4 Anemia

Children with CRF develop increasing anemia as a result of erythropoietin (EPO) deficiency. If therapy is not introduced in time, hemoglobin values of around 50 g/l are usual in the terminal stages of renal failure. It is not certain if, or to what extent, chronic anemia leads to growth impairment. Children with chronic anemia (e.g. thalassemia major) show retardation of growth and development. When treated with high-frequency transfusion regimens to keep hematocrits close to the normal range, growth rates may improve in these patients [78]. Theoretically, anemia may interfere with growth via various mechanisms, such as poor appetite, intercurrent infections, cardiac complications and poor oxygenation of cartilage cells in the growth plate. The introduction of recombinant EPO for the treatment of renal anemia has offered the opportunity to study whether changes in growth are induced by the compensation of renal anemia. Whereas short-term stimulatory effects of EPO have been observed in single patients [79], no persistent effect was observed in prospective trials [80]. Likewise, blood transfusion and EPO treatment of uremic rats did not result in improved growth [81].

3.5 Renal osteodystrophy

Renal osteodystrophy is caused by a renal disorder in vitamin D metabolism and by secondary hyperparathyroidism. Following unsuccessful prevention or inadequate treatment, osteodystrophy clinically manifests as skeletal deformities, muscular hypotension and, occasionally, as slipped epiphyses. Histologically, the condition presents as a mixture of osteomalacia and osteitis fibrosa, sometimes with one of the components almost completely predominating. In contrast to vitamin D deficiency rickets, in renal osteodystrophy the radiological changes in the growth plate and metaphysis are caused by the transformation of the primary spongiosa into fibrous tissue and woven bone rather than by the persistence of non-calcified growth cartilage (Fig. 9).

Although gross skeletal deformities can contribute to the retardation of a child's growth, the appearance of renal osteodystrophy is not inevitably paralleled by alterations in epiphyseal growth of the long bones. Severe metaphyseal skeletal changes are often detected radiologically in patients with relatively good growth rates. In such cases, osteopathy is unmasked by rapid growth. Growth is arrested completely only

| Control | Vitamin D deficiency rickets | Renal osteodystrophy |

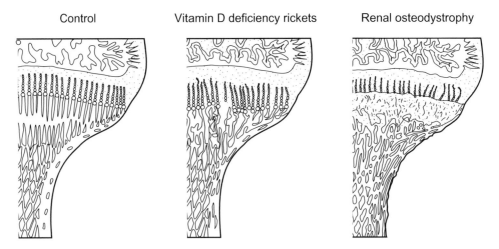

Fig. 9. *Schematic representation of the metaphyseal changes in rickets and renal osteodystrophy. The widening of the growth plate in vitamin D deficiency rickets (centre) results from a broadening of the growth cartilage zone as a consequence of the persistence of chondrocytes and impaired primary calcification. In renal osteodystrophy (right), the widening is caused by the appearance of fibrochondroclastic and fibro-osteoclastic tissue and woven bone. This leads to a narrowing of the cartilage layer and to the breakdown of primary spongiosa. The complete breakdown of the growth plate architecture can lead to slipping of epiphyses and cessation of growth.*

From [82] with permission.

when secondary hyperparathyroidism results in severe destruction of the metaphyseal bone architecture.

Whereas treatment with vitamin D and 1,25-dihydroxyvitamin D_3 (1,25$(OH)_2D_3$) improves growth in uremic rats [83], equivalent therapeutic success has not been achieved in children with CRF. Treatment with 5000 to 10 000 IU vitamin D_3 per day did not affect growth in dialyzed children [84]. An early optimistic report in four patients receiving 1,25$(OH)_2D_3$ [85] could not be validated in the long term [86]. This therapeutic failure contrasts with the remarkable growth improvement in patients treated for vitamin D deficiency rickets, in whom a similar disorder of renal vitamin D metabolism without renal failure is present.

The extent to which secondary hyperparathyroidism contributes to growth impairment is unclear. Parathyroid hormone (PTH) is an anabolic hormone and an intrinsic growth factor, stimulating mitosis in osteoprogenitor cells and growth plate chondrocytes and up-regulating the vitamin D receptor [87, 88]. Intermittent but not continuous administration of PTH stimulates skeletal growth in normal and uremic rats [89]. However, resistance to the effect of PTH is observed in uremia, characterized by reduced cAMP production in growth plate chondrocytes [87]. Low bone turnover induced by relatively low PTH levels may contribute to growth impairment [90]. At the other end of the spectrum, excessive secretion of PTH can lead to the destruction of growth plate architecture [91], epiphyseal displacement [92] and metaphyseal fractures [93].

3.6 Renal transplantation

In principle, successful renal transplantation restores the conditions for normal growth compromised by the state of uremia. However, published experience of post-transplant growth varies widely, ranging from a steady continuing deterioration of relative height to nearly complete catch-up growth. One of the main factors responsible for this diversity is the variability of immunosuppression. As outlined in Chapter 4 (page 52; *Interactions between glucocorticoids and the GH/IGF axis*) and in Chapter 5 (page 73; *Growth plate disturbances as a consequence of glucocorticoid therapy*), corticosteroids suppress growth mainly by interacting with the GH/IGF-I axis and by their direct effects on the growth plate. The second main factor influencing growth is graft function. The growth-suppressive effect of poor graft function is independent of the usually higher dosage of corticosteroids administered to patients with CRF. Age and the degree of growth retardation at the time of transplantation have been identified

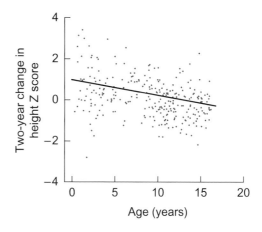

Fig. 10. *Change in standardized height during the first 2 years after transplantation. Improvement in mean height Z score is limited to children of pre-school age.*

From [94] with permission.

as further significant predictors of post-transplant growth [94] (Fig. 10).

3.7 Hormonal factors

Apart from the impairment of $1,25(OH)_2D_3$ and PTH secretion mentioned above, disorders of hormone regulation have been described in virtually all the hormone systems involved in growth. Hormonal resistance, despite elevated levels mainly due to diminished renal elimination, seems to be a major pathogenetic principle. Details of the derangement of several hormonal axes are reported in Chapter 4.

4 Endocrine abnormalities in chronic renal failure

Summary

Endocrine function is disturbed in chronic renal failure (CRF), with uremia affecting the regulation of both renal and extrarenal hormones. In addition to changes in gonadal function, patients with CRF have altered levels of circulating gonadal hormones and gonadotropins. These hormonal changes are usually normalized after successful renal transplantation, indicating that regulatory mechanisms, rather than toxic end-organ damage, affect gonadal function in uremia. Disturbances in the somatotropic hormone axis play a major role in growth retardation and catabolism in children with CRF. Growth hormone (GH) insensitivity in patients with CRF may reflect reductions in the circulating levels of insulin-like growth factor I (IGF-I) and GH-binding protein, disturbed signaling of the GH receptor, as well as the progressive increase in levels of IGF-binding proteins. GH therapy exerts the majority of its stimulatory effects on growth by increasing serum IGF-I levels, as well as by altering the relative quantities of certain IGF-binding proteins. Supraphysiological doses of GH produce a rapid and persistent increase in IGF levels in children with CRF. GH may also be used to counter the growth-suppressing effects of long-term high-dose glucocorticoid medication, producing not only improved growth, but reduced protein catabolism and osteoporosis. Thyroid and adrenal disorders are difficult to diagnose in patients with CRF, as the clinical features can be indistinguishable from those of uremia. An evaluation of thyroid and adrenal hormonal status should be carried out in patients with CRF to screen for endocrine disturbances.

4.1 Mechanisms of endocrine abnormalities

Uremia interferes with metabolism and regulation of hormones by various mechanisms. In principle, disturbed endocrine function may arise either from inappropriate circulating hormone concentrations or from changed hormonal action at the target tissue level. Both conditions may be present in the uremic state.

Increased plasma hormone concentrations

Renal catabolism accounts for a major part of the metabolic clearance rates of various peptide hormones [95]. Most polypeptide hormones are almost freely filtered in the glomerulus, followed by either intratubular (brush border peptidases) or intracellular (cytosolic or lysosomal) degradation in tubular cells. Moreover, certain hormones are subject to receptor-mediated uptake across the basolateral tubular cell membrane. If catabolic mechanisms differ for different isoforms or subunits of a hormone, an imbalance of these constituents may arise, altering the relationship between biologically active and inactive hormone fragments. Besides renal metabolic clearance, extrarenal hormone elimination may be reduced in renal failure. For example, degradation of insulin in skeletal muscle tissue is diminished [96], and hepatic catabolism of biologically active PTH is reduced in uremia [97].

In addition to reductions in hormone clearance, hypersecretion of various hormones or hormone-binding proteins occurs in renal failure, either as an appropriate response to secretory stimuli (e.g. PTH) or without an apparent homeostatic signal (e.g. prolactin).

Decreased plasma hormone concentrations

The reduction in functional renal mass is assumed to be the main cause of decreased levels of hormones produced by the kidney (EPO, $1,25(OH_2)D_3$). In addition, the uremic milieu may suppress the production of these hormones. For example, intracellular phosphate accumulation may inhibit 1α-hydroxylase even before the reduction of renal mass becomes quantitatively important. Levels of extrarenal hormones may be decreased when the hormone-producing gland is the final effector organ of a complex hormonal axis (e.g. testis–testosterone,

ovary–estradiol). In these cases, insufficient production of hormones may result from direct toxic damage to the endocrine gland, from insufficient stimulatory input from the superior part of the hormonal axis or from hyporesponsiveness of the gland.

Disorders of hormone action
Disturbed conversion of prohormones to hormones

Concentrations of certain prohormones are elevated in CRF; for example, pro-IGF-IA, a precursor of IGF-I, which is not detectable in normal serum [98], or proinsulin, which is not converted appropriately to insulin or C-peptide in patients with ESRD [99]. Peripheral conversion of thyroxine (T_4) to tissue-active tri-iodothyronine (T_3) is impaired [100]. Some prohormones may block hormone action by competitively inhibiting receptor binding at the tissue level.

Shifts in the isohormone spectrum

Some polypeptide hormones circulate in plasma in multiple isoforms characterized by varying composition of their carbohydrate side chains. In uremia, certain low molecular weight degradation products of low bioactivity accumulate (e.g. glucagon). In addition, altered glycosylation [101] may shift the isohormone spectrum towards less bioactive forms (e.g. luteinizing hormone (LH)) [102].

Alterations of hormone-binding plasma proteins

Altered concentrations of, and/or affinity for, circulating binding proteins explain part of the alterations in the actions of somatotropic hormones in uremia. Whereas low levels of circulating GH-binding protein (GHBP) are believed to reflect down-regulation of GH receptor expression in the target tissue [103], increased levels of some of the IGF-I-binding proteins probably result in reduced bioavailability of IGF-I [104, 105].

Alterations of target tissue sensitivity
Reduced responsiveness of target tissues to endocrine signals, exemplified by the disturbed action of insulin on fat and muscle cells, or by the resistance of Leydig cells to human chorionic gonadotropin (HCG), may be explained by reduced receptor density and abnormal hormone–receptor interaction due to the presence of competitive or non-competitive inhibitory substances and/or structural changes of either the hormone or its receptor. Alternatively, impaired responsiveness of target tissues may result from alterations of hormone-dependent intracellular processes. Such post-receptor events seem to play a key role in the pathogenesis of the insulin resistance seen in uremia [106] (Fig. 11).

4.2 Gonadotropic hormone axis
Gonadal hormones
In adults with CRF, plasma concentrations of testosterone are usually low or low-normal [107], due to reduced synthesis and, perhaps, to an increased metabolic clearance rate [108, 109]. In prepubertal children with predialytic renal failure, low plasma concentrations of total and free testosterone and dihydrotestosterone (DHT) have been reported [110]. However, as the adrenal cortex is the major site of androgen production before puberty, and specific adrenal androgens are also low in children with CRF [108], low prepubertal levels of plasma androgen do not provide

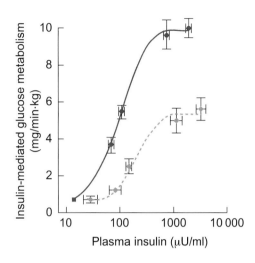

Fig. 11. *Dose–response relationship between the plasma insulin concentration and insulin-mediated glucose metabolism in patients with CRF (dashed line) and controls (solid line). Diminished maximal insulin-mediated glucose metabolism suggests insulin resistance by a post-receptor defect.*
From [106] with permission.

evidence for gonadal damage before puberty [111, 112]. In pubertal patients, normal or slightly subnormal plasma testosterone concentrations are observed [113–117]. In late puberty, however, DHT concentrations are significantly reduced in children with CRF compared with healthy or post-transplant children (authors' unpublished observations). Impaired conversion of testosterone to DHT due to decreased 5α-reductase activity has been suggested [118, 119]. Because this metabolite is responsible for many tissue actions of androgens, reduced conversion of testosterone to DHT may explain the frequently reduced development of secondary sexual characteristics in boys with advanced renal failure.

The testicular response to supra-physiological stimulation by HCG is impaired in adult men [107] as well as in prepubertal and pubertal boys with CRF. Testicular insufficiency is most prominent in boys on hemodialysis [113]. Leydig cell resistance is caused by a cAMP-dependent mechanism [120]. Recently, the presence of an endogenous LH receptor inhibitor in uremic serum has been demonstrated [121] (Fig. 12). The disorder is reversed by renal transplantation [113].

The physiological age-related decrease of sex-hormone-binding globulin is conserved in prepubertal children on dialysis [116]; at a given age, however, sex-hormone-binding globulin concentrations are higher and the unbound testosterone fraction is lower than in normal children. The increase in sex-hormone-binding globulin may be due to accumulation in ESRD; a normal fraction of free testosterone has been reported in prepubertal children with compensated CRF on conservative treatment [110].

The plasma concentration of inhibin, a polypeptide produced by the Sertoli and granulosa cells, is elevated in peripubertal boys with CRF [122]. It is as yet unclear whether elevated levels of plasma inhibin in uremia reflect alterations of Sertoli cell function, impaired feedback regulation of the pituitary–gonadal axis or decreased metabolic clearance of the hormone.

Plasma concentrations of estradiol in the low-normal range are observed in women with CRF [123, 124]. In pubertal girls with CRF, plasma levels of estradiol were normal or low when related to pubertal stage [125, 126]. An inverse correlation between serum creatinine levels and estradiol concentrations was found in patients with predialytic CRF. Longitudinal

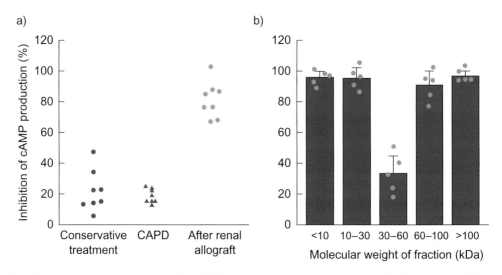

Fig. 12. Evidence for circulating LH inhibitor in sera of uremic boys. (a) HCG-induced cAMP production by a cell line expressing human LH/HCG receptor is suppressed in the presence of serum from patients on conservative treatment or continuous ambulatory peritoneal dialysis (CAPD). (b) Inhibitory activity of uremic serum is confined to a fraction containing 30–60 kDa proteins.

Adapted from [121] with permission.

analysis revealed an insufficient increase in estradiol during puberty in those patients whose renal function deteriorated, whereas following renal transplantation, even after several years of dialysis, estradiol concentrations increased [126].

Gonadotropins

Plasma LH levels are high-normal or elevated in adult men [107] and women [123, 124, 127] and in prepubertal and pubertal boys [102, 110, 128] and girls [102, 110, 125] with CRF; follicle-stimulating hormone (FSH) concentrations are also usually elevated both in adults and children with CRF. After transplantation, LH levels usually return to normal, whereas plasma levels of FSH frequently remain elevated.

The combination of elevated gonadotropins with decreased or low-normal gonadal hormone levels has been taken as evidence for a state of compensated hypergonadotropic hypogonadism [110, 129]. However, the degree of hypergonadotropism in CRF is usually inadequate for the prevailing degree of hypogonadism, suggesting an additional defect of hypophyseal gonadotropin secretion.

An alteration at the pituitary level is suggested by the blunted increase of plasma LH and FSH following stimulation by a bolus of exogenous gonadotropin-releasing hormone (GnRH) in men, women [107], boys [110, 114] and girls [125] with CRF. These abnormalities appear even more marked when the diminished metabolic clearance of gonadotropins [130] is taken into account. The gonadotropin response to GnRH is normalized after successful transplantation [125].

LH is released from the pituitary in episodic (pulsatile) bursts occurring every 90–120 minutes. The peaks in plasma LH concentrations reflect intermittent secretion of hypothalamic GnRH into the hypophyseal–portal bloodstream [131]. Hence, the analysis of plasma LH pulses gives indirect information about the functional state of the hypothalamic GnRH 'pacemaker'. Differentiation of the secretion and elimination components underlying the fluctuating plasma LH concentration patterns by means of deconvolution analysis [132] revealed that the elevation of basal plasma LH concentrations is due entirely to the diminished renal metabolic clearance of the hormone [130] both in humans [133] and in rats [134]. The plasma half-life of LH is inversely correlated with GFR [133]. In contrast, actual pituitary LH secretion rates are decreased in CRF; pubertal patients on dialysis secrete three times less immunoreactive LH and 2.5 times less bioactive LH in episodic nocturnal peaks than normal adolescents [133] (Fig. 13). This abnormality, which has been reproduced in experimental uremia [135], provides strong evidence for a dysregulation of the gonadotropic axis at the hypothalamo-pituitary level. After transplantation, a regular pattern of LH pulses is re-established [102, 136]. As the onset of puberty is heralded by the emergence of a nocturnal pattern of pulsatile LH secretion, the observed disturbance of pulsatile LH secretion suggests that the delayed pubertal development in CRF is caused by a primary hypothalamic defect. Experimental evidence confirms that the subnormal pituitary gonadotropin secretion is caused by diminished release of GnRH into the hypophyseal–portal circulation [134, 137]. In cultured GnRH-producing neurons,

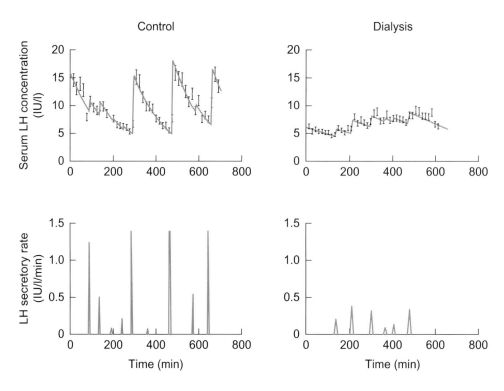

Fig. 13. *Nocturnal plasma concentration profiles of bioactive LH in a normal midpubertal boy (left panel) and a midpubertal boy on hemodialysis (right panel). Upper panels show original LH concentrations and the fitted curve; the lower panels show estimated hormone secretion rates. As a result of a prolonged plasma hormone half-life and reduced pituitary secretion rate, the dialysis patient exhibits an apparently non-pulsatile plasma concentration pattern.*

Adapted from [133] with permission.

inhibition of GnRH release has been observed upon addition of a high molecular weight fraction of uremic serum. Further investigation suggested that the inhibitor is a hydrophilic protein that suppresses GnRH exocytosis but not synthesis [138] (Fig. 14). Moreover, using *in vivo* intracerebral microdialysis in experimentally uremic rats, we observed an increased tone of the neuroinhibitory amino acid GABA in the extracellular fluid of the hypothalamic medial preoptic area, the region where the GnRH neurons reside [139] (Fig. 15). Hence, central nervous GABA accumulation may be another mechanism of down-regulation of the gonadotropic hormone axis in uremia.

In summary, clinical and experimental evidence indicate that the neuroendocrine control of pulsatile LH secretion is altered in CRF. Although overt hypogonadotropism is masked by a simultaneous reduction of metabolic clearance rates, the deficient physiological pulsatile GnRH–LH signal may be the key abnormality underlying the delayed onset of puberty in chronic renal disease. The observed disorders of LH secretion and metabolism appear

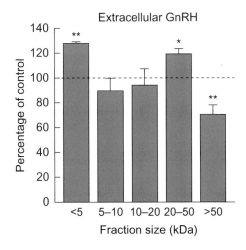

Fig. 14. *Selective inhibition of GnRH release from cultured neurons of a hypothalamic cell line (GT1-7) by incubation with a high molecular weight fraction of uremic serum. GnRH supernatant concentrations observed with serum fractions from control animals were defined as 100%.*

* p < 0.05; ** p < 0.01.

> *Adapted from [138] with permission.*

to be reversible after successful renal transplantation.

Besides the quantitative insufficiency of the hypothalamo-pituitary unit, the biological quality of the circulating gonadotropins is also altered in uremia. LH bioactivity, measured by the potency of a plasma sample to induce testosterone production in a Leydig cell culture, depends on the degree of glycosylation and sialylation of this glycoprotein hormone [140]. During normal puberty, the relative bioactivity of LH gradually increases [141]. In pubertal [142, 143] and adult patients [136] on dialysis, the ratio of bioactive to immunoreactive plasma LH is reduced, suggesting that the spectrum of circulating

LH molecules is shifted towards bioinactive forms [102, 133, 136, 144]. This may be attributed to altered glycosylation of plasma proteins in uremia [101]. The physiological increase in hormone bioactivity during puberty is absent in dialysis patients [143]. The recently characterized inhibitor of LH action circulating in serum of uremic boys may represent an accumulating LH fragment [121] (Fig. 12). After successful renal transplantation, LH biopotency tends to normalize.

Prolactin

Prolactin is a peptide hormone secreted by the pituitary and is involved in the regulation

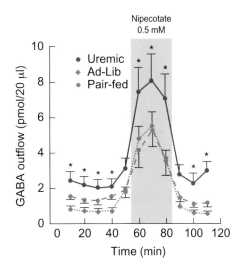

Fig. 15. *GABA outflow from the hypothalamic medial preoptic area during an in vivo microdialysis study in awake, unrestrained rats. Increased extracellular GABA concentrations were seen in animals with CRF before and during perfusion with GABA re-uptake inhibitor nipecotic acid.*
*Uremic rats differ from ad-libitum (Ad-Lib) fed controls (p < 0.05).

> *Adapted from [139] with permission.*

of lactation. Its function in non-puerperal women, in men and in children is not clear. However, prolactin attenuates gonadotropin release. Plasma prolactin levels are elevated in men [145] and, more markedly, in women and pubertal girls [125, 145] with CRF. Uremic hyperprolactinemia appears to result from both a decreased metabolic clearance rate and an increased production rate of the hormone [146]. Hyperprolactinemia may play a role in the pathogenesis of uremic hypogonadism, as elevated prolactin levels exert a suppressive effect on the GnRH–LH pulse generator [147]. The physiological sleep-related nocturnal prolactin surge is absent [148] and the circadian rhythm of secretion is deranged [149] in CRF. Prolactin secretion in CRF patients is insensitive to stimulation by thyrotropin-releasing hormone (TRH) [150], chlorpromazine, metoclopramide, arginine or insulin-induced hypoglycemia [151]. L-Dopa and dopamine are not effective in suppressing prolactin secretion [151]; however, hyperprolactinemia may be corrected by long-term treatment with dopaminergic agonists [152, 153]. Uremic hyperprolactinemia may be related to other complications of CRF; these include vitamin D deficiency and renal anemia. Substitution of $1,25(OH_2)D_3$ [154] and EPO [155] leads to partial normalization of plasma prolactin levels.

Conclusion

Various physiological studies and pharmacological tests reveal a partial disintegration of the gonadotropic hormone axis at the hypothalamo-pituitary level, in addition to alterations of gonadal function. The analysis of hormone secretory patterns has confirmed that the central nervous dysregulation is not restricted to the functional reserve capacity

of the reproductive hormone system, but affects physiological spontaneous hormone secretion. The reversibility of the observed changes after successful renal transplantation gives further evidence that regulatory mechanisms, rather than toxic end-organ damage, affect gonadal function in uremia. Future investigations will have to delineate to what extent the apparent 'dysregulation' of hormone secretion represents a 'physiological' adaptation to disturbed hormone secretion.

4.3 Disturbances of the GH/IGF axis
Physiology of the GH/IGF axis and the somatomedin hypothesis

GH exerts its somatotropic effects partially by stimulating the production of IGF-I (Fig. 16a). Circulating IGF-I, mainly derived from the liver, acts as a classic endocrine hormone, whereas IGF-I produced locally in the growth cartilage acts as a paracrine/autocrine growth factor [156]. According to the dual-effector theory [157], both hormones act on different cell types for the stimulation of longitudinal growth. GH induces differentiation of epiphyseal growth plate precursor cells toward chondrocytes, and these GH-stimulated chondrocytes become responsive to IGF-I and concomitantly express IGF-I mRNA. IGF-I, on the other hand, stimulates the clonal expansion of differentiated chondrocytes, thus leading to longitudinal bone growth [158]. In addition to GH, circulating as well as locally produced IGF-I is regulated by the nutritional status [159–161]. Both protein and calorie intake have been identified as relevant permissive factors, which regulate IGF-I production either by a decrease of GH receptor density or by post-receptor

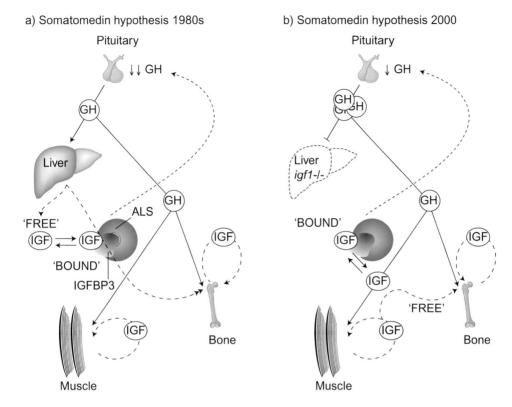

Fig. 16. *(a) The somatomedin hypothesis in the 1980s and (b) the revised somatomedin hypothesis according to recent gene deletion experiments that have questioned the role of hepatic IGF-I and the bound form of circulating IGF-I in controlling postnatal growth and development.*

Adapted from [156], with permission.

mechanisms [161, 162]. Sex steroids raise circulating IGF-I levels during puberty mainly through regulation of GH secretion [163]. The regulation and physiological significance of IGF-II for postnatal growth is less well defined.

Recent studies have revealed the endocrine GH/IGF-I system to be considerably more complex, involving multiple level interactions between circulating and tissue IGF-binding proteins (IGFBPs). Observations of near-normal growth in mice with liver-specific IGF-I deletions [164, 165] and deletion of the acid-labile subunit (ALS) [166], which forms a ternary complex with IGFBP-3 and IGF-I in the circulation, have questioned the role of circulating IGF-I in somatic growth. It has been hypothesized that somatic growth is due primarily to GH-stimulated locally produced IGF-I, while IGF-I in the circulation serves mainly to provide systemic negative feedback on GH secretion (Fig. 16b). Rather than acting to promote growth, circulating IGF-I might actually restrain the somatotropic axis. However, most of the evidence for GH-stimulated local IGF-I production comes from rodents.

In humans, there is generally a good correlation between circulating IGF-I levels and somatic growth. Furthermore, treating patients with GH insensitivity systemically with IGF-I produces nearly normal growth. The failure of IGF-I treatment to achieve fully normal growth in GH-resistant children may be due to inadequate exposure to IGF-I as, in the absence of a GH effect, formation of the ternary complex is impaired and IGF-I is rapidly cleared from the circulation. Alternatively, specific GH effects on the growth plate, as proposed in the dual-effector theory, may be required for optimal growth. However, there are some examples of near-normal growth in humans despite low GH levels, but with normal circulating IGF-I levels [167, 168]. Our current view of the regulation of postnatal somatic growth therefore includes both the endocrine actions of IGF-I, modulated by GH-induced and GH-independent IGFBP complexes, and a local mode of action involving direct effects of both GH and IGF-I and possibly IGF-II at the growth plate (Fig. 16). Finally, IGF-I has GH-independent actions in embryonic growth and in reproductive system function.

Disturbances of the GH/IGF axis in CRF

GH

Random fasting serum levels of GH are normal or increased in children and adults

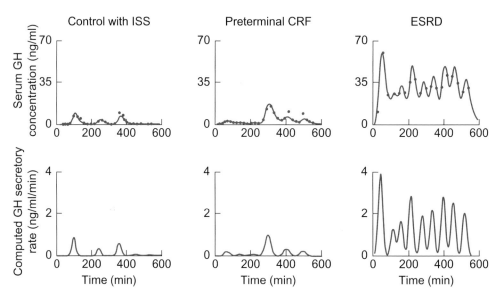

Fig. 17. *Illustrative profiles of pulsatile plasma GH concentrations in one subject with idiopathic short stature (ISS), one child with preterminal CRF and one child with ESRD. The upper panels depict the serial plasma GH concentrations over time, as measured by immunoradiometric assay of plasma derived from blood collected at 20-minute intervals for 10 hours, and the deconvolution-predicted curves, which closely approximate the experimental data points. The lower panels show the deconvolution-calculated GH secretory bursts over a period of 10 hours. Note the presence of an increased number of secretory bursts in the child with ESRD.*

From [173] with permission.

with CRF, depending on the extent of renal failure [169–171]. For the interpretation of these data, information about the secretory pattern of GH, such as the specific physiological regulation of the frequency and amplitude of pulsatile GH secretion, and its metabolic clearance is important. This is particularly the case in patients with CRF, because the kidney accounts for a substantial fraction of the serum turn-over of GH [172]. The application of deconvolution analysis has permitted indirect calculation of pituitary GH secretion, independent of the metabolic clearance of the hormone. By use of this methodology, the GH secretion rate from the pituitary in CRF was found to be variable between patients and studies. A high-normal calculated GH secretion rate and an amplified number of GH secretory bursts were reported in prepubertal children with ESRD, presumably as a result of attenuated bioactive IGF-I feedback of the somatotropic axis (Fig. 17) [173]. In adult patients on hemodialysis, the GH secretion rate was clearly elevated [174], whereas in pubertal patients with advanced CRF, reduced GH secretion rates were observed, indicating an altered sensitivity of the somatotropic hormone axis to the stimulatory effect of sex steroids, at least in this developmental stage [175]. The apparent variability in the calculated GH secretion rates in these studies may be due to differences in age and nutritional status of the study populations, parameters which strongly influence spontaneous GH secretion. A prolonged GH half-life due to a decreased metabolic clearance rate resulting from a reduction in functional renal mass was a consistent finding in all studies [173–175]. The concept that the kidneys account for a substantial fraction of the serum turnover of

GH in humans is supported by data from an infusion study with GH. This demonstrated a 50% reduced metabolic clearance rate of GH both in children and adults with CRF, which correlated with the residual renal function (Fig. 18) [176].

The apparent discrepancy between normal or elevated GH serum levels and diminished longitudinal growth in children with CRF has led to the concept of insensitivity to the action of GH in the uremic state. It is noteworthy that GH insensitivity is associated with clinical and experimental CRF in the absence of concomitant metabolic acidosis or malnutrition, although these two factors are potentially aggravating. This 'uremic' GH insensitivity is due to multiple derangements of distal components of the somatotropic hormone axis that are described below.

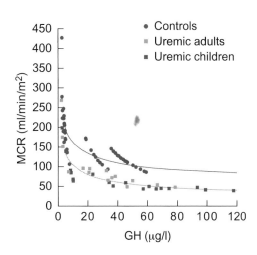

Fig. 18. *Total metabolic clearance rate (MCR) as a function of steady-state plasma GH concentrations in controls and uremic subjects. Total MCR was expressed as a power function of steady-state GH concentrations in controls (dark line) and in uremic patients (pale line).*
From [176] with permission.

GH receptor/GHBP

One molecular mechanism for the peripheral insensitivity to the action of GH in CRF is a reduced density of GH receptors in GH target organs. In humans, the circulating high-affinity GHBP is thought to reflect GH receptor expression because it is produced by a limited proteolytic cleavage of the GH receptor and release of the extracellular domain into the circulation [177]. Determination of serum GHBP concentrations may be used to assess GH receptor density in tissues, particularly in the liver, because circulating GHBP is believed to derive mainly, but not exclusively, from liver tissue. GHBP activity in serum is low in children [103, 178] and adults [179–181] with CRF. In a large analysis of 126 children with CRF, serum GHBP concentrations were below the mean for age- and gender-matched controls in 77% of CRF patients (Fig. 19) [178]. The decrease of age- and gender-adjusted serum GHBP levels is related to the degree of renal dysfunction; children with ESRD have the lowest GHBP levels (–2.25 ± 0.22 SDS). In this study [178], the vast majority (91%) of children with CRF had a BMI within the normal range. Nevertheless, BMI, rather than the degree of renal dysfunction, was the prevailing determinant of serum GHBP levels in these children, indicating that variations in nutritional status within the normal range are an important determinant of GH receptor status in tissues.

The decreased GHBP/GH receptor status in children with CRF has functional relevance with respect to growth. Serum GHBP is correlated with both the spontaneous growth rate (Fig. 20) and the growth response to GH therapy in children with CRF (Fig. 21); baseline GHBP levels predict approximately 30% of the growth response to GH treatment in these patients [178]. Hence, GHBP levels serve as an indicator of sensitivity to both endogenous

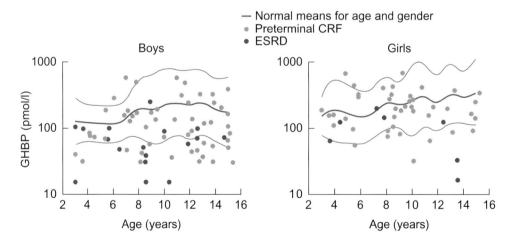

Fig. 19. *Serum GHBP concentrations in 75 boys and 51 girls with CRF related to the age- and gender-dependent normal range (–2 to +2 SDS). The bold line indicates the normal mean for age and gender. Pale circles represent children with preterminal CRF, dark circles children with ESRD receiving dialysis.*

Adapted from [178] with permission.

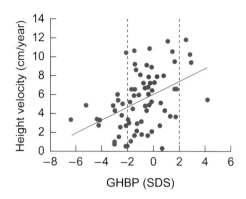

Fig. 20. *Spontaneous height velocity in 75 prepubertal children with CRF as a function of age- and gender-related serum GHBP levels. The normal range for GHBP (–2 to +2 SDS) is indicated by the dotted lines. There was a significant positive correlation (r = 0.44, p < 0.0001).*

From [178] with permission.

and exogenous GH and may be a useful clinical parameter to predict the growth response to GH. These observations also help to explain the lower growth response to exogenous GH in children with ESRD compared with that in children with residual renal function, because serum GHBP/GH receptor status is suppressed most in the former group [178].

Is low tissue GH receptor density in CRF the reason or the consequence of high plasma levels of GH in advanced CRF? Most clinical and experimental data argue against direct regulation of GH receptors by endogenous GH *in vivo*. In the majority of studies, children and adults with GH deficiency have normal serum GHBP levels [182–184] and these levels do not change during subcutaneous GH replacement therapy [183, 185, 186]. On the other hand, some patients with idiopathic short stature exhibit clearly decreased serum GHBP

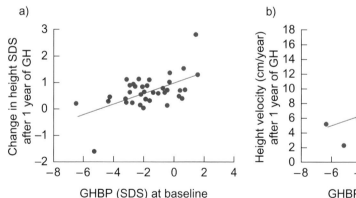

Fig. 21. *(a) Change in height SDS and (b) height velocity as a function of baseline age- and gender-related serum GHBP levels (SDS) in 40 prepubertal children with CRF, treated for 1 year with 28 IU GH/m² body surface area per week given as daily subcutaneous injections. There was a significant positive correlation: (a) r = 0.57, p < 0.0001; (b) r = 0.48, p < 0.005.*

From [178] with permission.

levels in the presence of normal GH secretion [182]. These results argue against a direct regulation of GHBP/GH receptors by GH. More likely is a direct suppressive effect of the uremic milieu on tissue GH receptor density, which leads to an adaptive increase in pituitary GH secretion, in addition to the diminished feedback down-regulation of GH secretion by decreased IGF bioactivity [173, 174].

In concordance with these finding, a significant reduction of hepatic GH receptor mRNA abundance, which was nutrition independent, has been described in non-acidotic experimental uremia in the 5/6 nephrectomy rat model in most [187, 188] but not all [189] studies. These findings

suggest that the relative insensitivity to the action of GH in uremia is partially due to a quantitative reduction of GH receptor density in GH target organs, particularly in the liver. The specific metabolic signal of the uremic milieu responsible for the low GHBP/GH receptor status in CRF remains to be elucidated. Acquired disease states associated with GH insensitivity, such as acute fasting, chronic malnutrition and insulin-dependent diabetes mellitus, also have reduced serum GHBP activity. In experimental uremia, subcutaneous GH treatment neither altered hepatic GH receptor transcript abundance nor serum GHBP levels [188]. Similarly, circulating GHBP levels in children with CRF did not

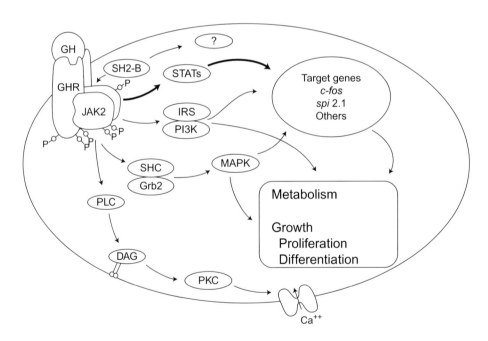

Fig. 22. *Possible signaling pathways initiated by binding of GH (GHR, GH receptor; P, phosphorylated tyrosines; JAK, Janus kinase; IRS, insulin receptor substrate; PI3K, phosphatidylinositol-3-kinase; PLC, phospholipase C; DAG, diacylglycerol; PKC, protein kinase C; MAPK, mitogen-activated protein kinase; STAT, signal transducer and activator of transcription).*

From [190] with permission.

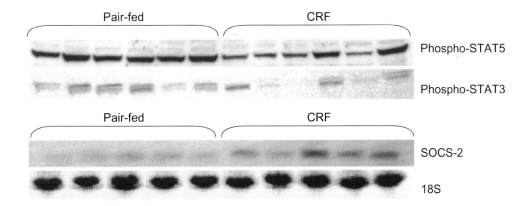

Fig. 23. Disturbed signaling events of the GH receptor. Deficient nuclear accumulation of tyrosine-phosphorylated STAT5 and STAT3 protein in rats with CRF compared with pair-fed control animals (upper panel). The mRNA abundance of suppressor of cytokine signaling (SOCS)-2 in GH-treated rats with CRF is increased (lower panel). SOCS-2 inhibits STAT phosphorylation by binding to tyrosine kinase JAK2.

From [189] with permission.

change during GH therapy [178]. Hence, the growth-promoting effect of GH, given subcutaneously, is not mediated by hepatic GH receptor up-regulation.

GH signaling

Recent evidence indicates that GH resistance in renal failure may be due, in part, to an acquired defect in the GH-activated Janus kinase 2 (JAK2) signal transducer and activator of transcription (STAT) pathway [189]. Normally, binding of GH to its receptor induces receptor dimerization, which is followed by autophosphorylation of JAK2, a tyrosine kinase associated with the intracellular domain of the receptor [190]. The activated JAK2, in turn, phosphorylates selective members of the STAT family of proteins, namely STAT1, STAT3, STAT5a and STAT5b. The phosphorylated STATs form dimers that translocate into the nucleus, bind to specific promoter sequences of GH-

dependent genes and transactivate or repress their transcription (Figs 22 and 23). Male mice with STAT5b deficiency and female mice with a combined deletion of STAT5a and STAT5b isoforms are severely growth retarded [191, 192]. A somewhat similar pattern of signaling events involving members of the JAK and STAT families occurs when other cytokines belonging to the cytokine/hemopoietin family bind to their specific receptors [193].

In uremic rats, hepatic GH receptor mRNA levels are significantly decreased, but GH receptor protein abundance and GH binding to microsomal and plasma membranes are unaltered. JAK2, STAT1, STAT3 and STAT5 protein abundance are also unchanged. However, GH-induced tyrosine phosphorylation of JAK2, STAT5 and STAT3 was found to be 75% lower in the uremic animals. Phosphorylated STAT5 and STAT3 were also diminished in nuclear extracts [189].

In the past few years, a family of proteins has been discovered that binds to cytokine receptor–JAK2 complexes and inhibits the kinase activity of JAK2 [194]. GH induces the expression of some of these suppressors of cytokine signaling (SOCS), namely SOCS-1, -2, -3 and cytokine-inducible SH2 protein (CIS), through the JAK–STAT signaling pathway. These suppressors, in turn, inhibit activation of the GH receptor–JAK2 complex or STAT5 phosphorylation, thus serving as a negative-feedback loop regulating GH activity [195–197]. Deletion of the SOCS-2 gene leads to gigantism in mice [198]. In experimental uremia, SOCS-2 and SOCS-3 mRNA levels increase [189] and, if followed by an increase in protein expression, could be a cause of the depressed JAK2–STAT activity. The mechanism accounting for the increase in SOCS mRNA levels in uremia, when GH-activated JAK2–STAT signaling is impaired, is somewhat of a puzzle. One potential mechanism could involve the action of cytokines that induce signal transduction through the activation of other members of the JAK family, such as JAK1, JAK3 and Tyk2, that may be unaffected by uremia [193]. It is also possible that the increase in SOCS expression in uremia might be mediated by GH through a non-STAT-mediated pathway [199]. Finally, it should be recognized that uremia impacts on several biologic processes, including gene stability and transcription, interaction between signaling pathways, and the action of a number of hormones and cytokines.

An acquired defect of GH-induced JAK–STAT signaling also occurs in inflammatory states [200, 201] that may arise from the overexpression of SOCS. Following administration of endotoxin, phospho-rylation of JAK2 is depressed even though GH receptor abundance is unchanged [200]. However, because of an increase in JAK2 protein levels, total phosphorylated JAK2 remains the same. Nevertheless, despite this compensation, downstream STAT5 phosphorylation is impaired. These changes are accompanied by an acute increase in SOCS-3 and CIS and, to a lesser degree, SOCS-2 expression. As chronic inflammation is common in patients with advanced kidney disease requiring dialysis treatment, it is conceivable that persistent inflammation with proinflammatory cytokine release may worsen the resistance to GH and thus play a role in the genesis of malnutrition, which is common in these patients [202].

IGF/IGFBP serum levels

The effect of GH on longitudinal growth is partially mediated by the IGFs. Serum IGF-I and IGF-II levels in children with preterminal CRF are in the normal range [203], whereas in ESRD mean age-related serum IGF-I levels are slightly, but significantly, decreased and IGF-II levels slightly, but significantly, elevated (Fig. 24) [204]. Hence, total immunoreactive IGF levels in CRF serum are normal, but IGF bioactivity, measured by sulfate incorporation into porcine costal cartilage, is markedly reduced [206, 207]. Similarly, the level of free IGF-I is reduced by 50% in relation to the degree of renal dysfunction [208]. This finding is one of the key abnormalities of the GH/IGF axis in children with CRF.

The discrepancy between normal total immunoreactive IGF levels and decreased IGF bioactivity has been explained by the presence of IGF inhibitors in CRF serum. Uremic serum contains low molecular weight

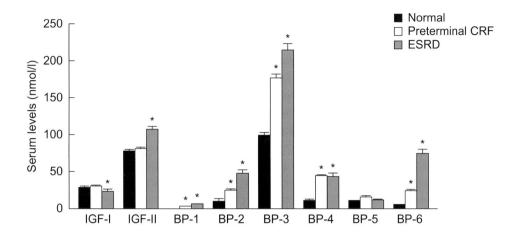

Fig. 24. *Comparison of the molar serum concentrations of IGFs and IGF-binding proteins (BP-1–BP-6) in children with preterminal CRF and children with ESRD. The mean molar concentrations in normal age-matched children are given for comparison. Data are mean + SEM.*
Significant versus control (p < 0.05).

From [205] with permission.

(about 1 kDa) IGF inhibitors, the molecular structures of which have not yet been defined [206]. The prevailing inhibitory effect on IGF bioactivity in CRF serum is due to an excess of high-affinity IGFBPs. Six IGFBPs have been distinguished on the basis of their amino acid sequences, which are encoded by different genes [209, 210]. The IGFBPs, which are proteins with an Mr of about 30 kDa and are named in the order of their molecular cloning, comprise a unique protein family. The IGFs circulate bound to IGFBPs in complexes of 150 kDa (major) and 35 kDa (minor). The 35 kDa serum fractions contain IGFBP-1, -2, -4 and -6, which are not found in the 150 kDa fractions. IGFBP-1 (28 kDa) is GH independent, and insulin is the principal suppressive regulator of hepatic IGFBP-1 production [211]. IGFBP-2 (32 kDa) is the second most abundant IGFBP in the circulation. It binds IGF-II with a greater affinity than IGF-I. IGFBP-1 and -2 are major contributors to the unsaturated IGFBP pool found primarily in the 35 kDa serum fraction [212, 213]. IGFBP-3, the most abundant serum IGFBP during extrauterine life, has many similarities to IGFBP-5:

- both can potentiate IGF action
- both are up-regulated by GH
- both are closely related structurally, sharing, among other motifs, an 18 amino acid heparin-binding domain that allows them to bind the ALS after binding either IGF-I or IGF-II. The subsequent constituted ternary complex has a molecular weight of approximately 150 kDa [214]. It is thought to function as a reservoir and a buffer for IGF-I and IGF-II, preventing rapid changes of free IGF levels.

Serum levels of intact IGFBP-1, -2 (Fig. 25), -4 (Fig. 26) and -6 are elevated in

CRF serum in relation to the degree of renal dysfunction [203, 205, 215–218]. These four IGFBPs, which have a high affinity for IGFs, are found in excess in the 35 kDa fractions of CRF serum. In contrast, serum levels of intact IGFBP-3 are normal, but there is an increase in immunoreactive low molecular weight fragments of IGFBP-3, in

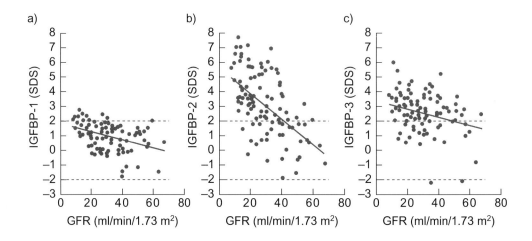

Fig. 25. Age-related serum (a) IGFBP-1, (b) IGFBP-2, and (c) IGFBP-3 levels as a function of GFR in children with CRF (n = 94). (a) r = –0.42, p < 0.001; (b) r = –0.56, p < 0.001; (c) r = –0.28, p < 0.005. The slope of the regression line between GFR and IGFBP-2 SDS was significantly steeper than that observed for IGFBP-1 and for IGFBP-3.

From [203] with permission.

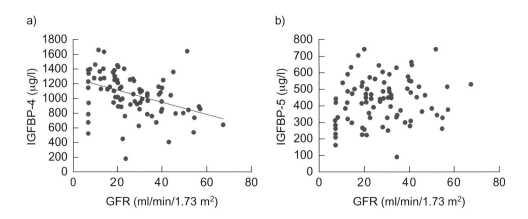

Fig. 26. Serum (a) IGFBP-4 and (b) IGFBP-5 as a function of GFR in children with CRF (n = 89). There was a significant inverse correlation between GFR and IGFBP-4 (r = –0.39, p < 0.001), but not IGFBP-5 (r = 0.16, p = 0.14).

From [205] with permission.

particular a 29 kDa fragment designated IGFBP-3[29] that has a reduced affinity for IGF peptides [219]. Levels of immuno-reactive IGFBP-5 are not altered in CRF serum (Fig. 26), but the majority of the IGFBP-5 is fragmented [214, 218].

Figure 24 shows the relative contribution of all six IGFBPs to the increased IGF-binding capacity of CRF serum. The relative increase of the respective serum IGFBPs in preterminal CRF ranges from 1.8-fold of control for immunoreactive IGFBP-3 to 4.8-fold for IGFBP-6. Taken together, there is approximately a 25% molar excess of IGFBPs over IGFs in the serum of healthy children, whereas in preterminal CRF the molar excess of IGFBPs over IGFs is approximately 150% and in ESRD 200% (Fig. 24). This estimation is in good agreement with the finding of a seven- to tenfold increase of free IGF-II binding capacity in the serum of children with preterminal CRF and ESRD, respectively [207]. In summary, these data demonstrate a progressive increase of serum IGFBPs in children with CRF in parallel with the decline of renal function. It is likely that the greater IGFBP excess in ESRD compared with preterminal CRF contributes both to more severe growth retardation and to the reduced response to GH therapy in these children [220].

IGF-I secretion

The pattern of normal serum IGF levels and markedly increased IGFBP levels is unique for CRF. The constellation of increased IGFBP over IGFs also suggests that 'normal' IGF-I and IGF-II levels in CRF cannot be interpreted as a consequence of normal production rates of these peptides. In CRF, IGF-binding capacity is increased by an order of magnitude [207]. Because of the short metabolic half-life of free IGF, one would expect that, under normal conditions, increased IGF-binding capacity would be immediately saturated by IGFs produced in the liver. The consequence would be a progressive increase of IGFs concomitantly with the rise in IGFBP as GFR declines. However, this tendency exists only for IGF-II [203]. Hence, the normal serum concentrations of IGF-I in preterminal CRF appear to be inadequately low. This discrepancy is even more pronounced in children with ESRD, in whom slightly decreased serum IGF-I levels are found in the presence of increased IGFBPs and in the presence of elevated circulating GH levels [173, 204]. Analysis of this complex system using a mathematical model indicated that data from children with CRF are consistent with a markedly reduced IGF-I production rate (Fig. 27) [221]. Consistent with this hypothesis, hepatic IGF-I gene expression in experimental uremia is reduced by 50% in non-acidotic animals compared with pair-fed controls [222]. This observation adds further evidence to the concept of GH insensitivity in the uremic state.

Mechanism of increased IGFBP levels in CRF serum

Theoretically, increased IGFBP levels in CRF serum could result from increased production, reduced transcapillary movement, reduced elimination by the diseased kidneys, or a combination of these factors. The inverse correlation of serum immunoreactive IGFBP-1, -2, -3, -4 and -6 with residual GFR in children with CRF is consistent with the concept that elevated IGFBPs result from impaired renal filtration. Similarly, there is a rapid decline of immunoreactive IGFBP-3 in

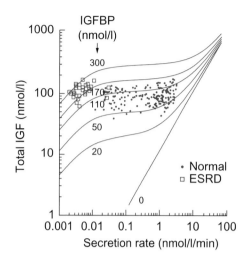

Fig. 27. Total IGF (IGF-I plus IGF-II) levels as a function of total secretion rate in the presence of various concentrations of IGFBP (0, 20, 50, 110, 170 and 300 nmol/l). The curves were calculated by a kinetic model. Values from normal individuals and from patients with ESRD were added to the graph according to their measured total IGF and IGFBP-3 concentrations.

Adapted from [221] with permission.

patients with ESRD after restoration of renal function by a functioning transplant [204]. Notably, increased proteolytic degradation of the IGFBP-3 ternary complex, as described during pregnancy and catabolic states, appears not to be operative in patients with CRF [223, 224]. The lack of increase in IGFBP-5 with progressive renal dysfunction has been interpreted as indirect evidence of reduced IGFBP-5 production in advanced CRF; because IGFBP-5 is a GH-responsive IGFBP, its production might be reduced as a consequence of GH insensitivity [205].

Increased hepatic production of IGFBP-1 and -2 appears to contribute to increased

IGFBP levels in CRF, as concluded from data in experimental uremia showing a twofold increase of IGFBP-1 mRNA and a fourfold increase of IGFBP-2 mRNA in liver tissue (Fig. 28) [222]. This alteration is tissue specific, because IGFBP-2 gene expression in kidney tissue is reduced in CRF. IGFBP-1 regulation is primarily transcriptional, with insulin being the major inhibitor of IGFBP-1 expression. Thus, the insulin resistance of CRF may contribute to high IGFBP-1 levels. The specific metabolic signal responsible for the marked increase of hepatic IGFBP-2 gene expression remains to be elucidated. Because IGFBP-2 mRNA levels are elevated in diabetic [225] and hypo-physectomized [226] rats, it has been suggested that insulin and GH are involved in the long-term regulation of hepatic IGFBP-2 gene expression. Insensitivity to the action of GH and insulin in uremic rats might therefore contribute to increased hepatic IGFBP-2 gene expression.

IGFBPs as modulators of IGF action *in vitro*

The prevailing inhibitory effect on IGF bioactivity in CRF serum is due to an excess of inhibitory IGFBPs. The removal of these unsaturated IGFBPs from CRF patient sera by affinity chromatography with an IGF-II Sepharose column restores IGF bioactivity in the porcine growth cartilage assay [207], indicating that unsaturated IGFBPs in CRF serum inhibit the ability of IGFs to act on cartilage tissue *in vitro*.

To inhibit IGF-mediated linear growth, IGFBPs must accumulate in extravascular fluids in sufficient quantity to block IGF effects on growth plate chondrocytes. IGFBP-1 and -2 and low molecular weight

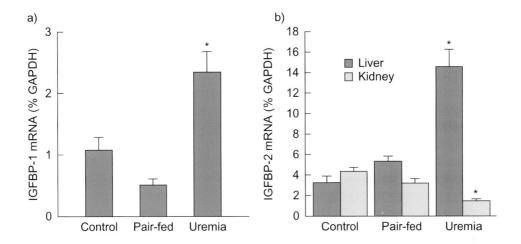

Fig. 28. *Quantification of (a) IGFBP-1 mRNA in liver and (b) IGFBP-2 mRNA in liver and kidney, quantified by Northern blot analysis. Values are expressed as the percentage of D-glyceraldehyde-3-phosphate dehydrogenase (GAPDH) expression.*
* Significant versus ad libitum-*fed controls and pair-fed controls.*

From [222] with permission.

forms of IGFBP-3 migrate into lymph fluid and thereby have access to interstitial spaces [227]. Levels of IGFBP-1 and -2 in extravascular fluids, such as lymph and peritoneal dialysate, are 10% of serum levels, or 2 nmol/l in the case of IGFBP-1 in the peritoneal dialysate of CRF children [228]. This concentration exceeds the 0.2 nmol IGFBP-1/l needed to inhibit basal growth of chick embryo pelvic cartilage in organ culture [229]. A molar excess of these high-affinity IGFBPs in IGF target tissues can therefore inhibit IGF action through their unsaturated IGF-binding sites, thereby preventing the interaction of IGFs with the type 1 IGF receptor.

The biological activity of various intact IGFBPs and their respective fragments from CRF serum has recently been studied systematically in the cartilage model of cultured growth plate chondrocytes (Table 3). IGFBP-1, -2 and -6 act exclusively as growth inhibitors on IGF-dependent proliferation of growth plate chondrocytes, whereas the biological activity of IGFBP-3 is complex. It has an IGF-independent antiproliferative effect and also inhibits IGF-dependent chondrocyte proliferation under co-incubation conditions. Under preincubation conditions, however, IGFBP-3 enhances the IGF-I responsiveness of growth plate chondrocytes by its ability to associate with the cell membrane, where it facilitates IGF-I receptor binding [232]. The IGFBP-3 fragment from CRF serum, IGFBP-3[29], has limited ability to inhibit IGF-II-mediated mitogenic effects, and no ability to inhibit IGF-I-mediated mitogenic effects, in cultured osteosarcoma cells, probably due to the low affinity of IGFBP-3 for IGF peptides [219]. IGFBP-4 and -5 have contrasting functions in growth

Table 3. *The concentration of intact IGFBPs and their respective fragments in CRF plasma, their intrinsic and IGF-dependent effect on growth plate chondrocyte proliferation, their correlation with parameters of longitudinal growth in children with CRF and the effect of their respective overexpression on growth in transgenic animals. References are in parentheses.*

IGFBP	Concentration in CRF plasma	Effect on growth plate chondrocyte proliferation[A]		Correlation to growth in clinical CRF	Growth in transgenic animals
		Intrinsic	IGF-dependent		
Intact IGFBP-1	Increased [203, 217]	None [232]	↓ [232]	Negative [203]	Pre-/postnatally reduced [234, 235]
Intact IGFBP-2	Increased [203, 217]	None [232]	↓ [232]	Negative [203, 217]	Postnatally reduced [236]
Intact IGFBP-3	Normal [216, 217]	↓ [232]	↓/↑[C] [232]	None[B] [203, 217]	Pre-/postnatally reduced [237]
IGFBP-3²⁹	Increased [219]	None[D] [219]	↓ (IGF-II)[D] [219]	ND	
Intact IGFBP-4	Increased [205, 218]	None [233]	↓ [233]	Negative[B] [205]	ND
IGFBP-4¹⁻¹²²	+ [230]	None [233]	↓ [233]	ND	
IGFBP-4¹³⁶⁻²³⁷	+ [230]	None [233]	None [233]	ND	
Intact IGFBP-5	Normal[B] [205, 218]	↑ [233]	↑ [233]	Positive[B] [205, 218]	ND
IGFBP-5¹⁻¹⁶⁹	ND	None [233]	↓ [233]	ND	
IGFBP-5¹⁴⁴⁻²⁵²	+ [231]	None [233]	None [233]	ND	
Intact IGFBP-6	Increased [215]	None [232]	↓ [232]	None [215]	ND

Abbreviations are: +, fragments present; ND, not done; ↓, inhibitory; ↑, stimulatory; [A]rat growth plate chondrocytes in primary culture; [B]immunoreactive IGFBP levels; [C]dependent on cell culture conditions; [D]human chondrosarcoma cells.

Adapted from Kiepe et al. Differential effects of IGFBP-1, -2, -3, and -6 on cultured growth plate chondrocytes. Kidney Int 2002;62(5):1591–6000 with permission.

plate chondrocytes [233]. Both intact IGFBP-4 and the fragment IGFBP-4¹⁻¹²² have an exclusive inhibitory role in IGF-I-stimulated cells by binding IGF-I in the *N*-terminal domain and preventing or reducing the binding of ligand to its signaling receptor. Intact IGFBP-5, on the other hand, stimulates chondrocyte proliferation, apparently by its association with the cell membrane in the *C*-terminal domain, thereby better presenting IGF-I to its receptor. However, if accumulated *N*-terminal forms of IGFBP-5 predominate, IGFBP-5 inhibits IGF-I-stimulated proliferation. This action of *N*-terminal IGFBP-5 in chondrocytes contrasts with its

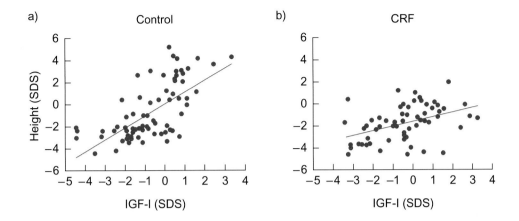

Fig. 29. *Age-related height SDS as a function of serum IGF-I levels (SDS) in (a) healthy prepubertal children and (b) prepubertal children with CRF (a) r = 0.67, p < 0.001; y = –0.006 + 1.08x. (b) r = 0.43, p < 0.001; y = –1.69 + 0.41x. The slope of the regression in children with CRF was significantly less steep than in controls. p < 0.001.*

From [203] with permission.

stimulatory effect on osteoblast activity and may be important in preserving the cartilage-to-bone developmental sequence that is necessary for normal longitudinal bone growth.

IGFBPs as modulators of IGF action *in vivo*

There is now direct evidence that circulating IGFBPs are capable of inhibiting growth in non-uremic experimental animals (Table 3). Co-injection of IGFBP-1 inhibited the GH- or IGF-I-stimulated weight gain and tibial epiphyseal widening of hypophysectomized rats in a dose-dependent manner [238]. In addition, transgenic mice overexpressing IGFBP-1 in multiple tissues or in liver alone are markedly growth retarded [234, 235]. Similarly, mice overexpressing IGFBP-2 show a reduced postnatal weight gain [236], and GH-stimulated growth is inhibited in giant GH transgenic mice overexpressing IGFBP-2 [239]. Overexpression of IGFBP-3

in transgenic mice, leading to a 4.9- to 7.7-fold increase in serum IGFBP-3 levels, produced modest intrauterine and postnatal growth retardation, despite elevated levels of circulating IGF-I [237]. This suggests that, *in vivo*, the inhibitory effects of excess IGFBP-3 on chondrocyte growth predominate over the modest growth-stimulatory effects observed with IGFBP-3 preincubation.

An important question is whether the imbalance between normal total IGF and the excess of unsaturated IGFBPs contributes to growth failure in the setting of clinical CRF. The normal relationship between circulating IGF-I and relative height is clearly disturbed in CRF (Fig. 29) [203]. The significantly less steep regression line between height and IGF-I in CRF is consistent with the presence of IGF inhibitors, indicating that the inhibition of IGF bioactivity for stimulation of longitudinal growth is also operative *in vivo*. Serum levels of IGFBP-1, -2 and -4

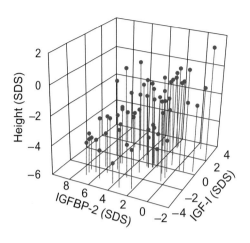

Fig. 30. Age-related height SDS in prepubertal children with CRF as a function of serum IGF-I levels (SDS) and IGFBP-2 levels (SDS). Height could be predicted from a linear combination of the independent variables IGF-I and IGFBP-2 (r = 0.54, p < 0.001 adjusted r² = 0.27).

From [203] with permission.

correlate significantly and inversely with standardized height in children with CRF, implying that these IGFBPs contribute to the growth failure in these children [203, 205, 217]. IGF-I (in a positive fashion) and IGFBP-2 (in a negative fashion) contribute independently to the statistical prediction of relative height in children with CRF (Fig. 30) [203]. The potential role of serum IGFBP-3 in longitudinal growth appears to be more complex. There is neither a positive relationship between immunoreactive IGFBP-3 and standardized height in CRF, as observed under normal conditions in healthy children, nor a negative correlation, which would be expected if IGFBP-3 acts merely as an IGF inhibitor in CRF [203]. On the other hand, GH therapy in CRF induced an increase in serum IGFBP-3 levels. This

correlated with improved growth in these children [217], suggesting a potential growth stimulatory effect of intact IGFBP-3 in this setting. These discrepant findings are probably due to the molecular heterogeneity of IGFBP-3 in CRF serum, comprising both intact IGFBP-3 and low molecular weight fragments, particularly IGFBP-3[29], with reduced IGF-binding capacity [219]. In contrast, serum IGFBP-5 levels are positively correlated with both standardized height and height velocity among children with CRF, consistent with a potential stimulatory role of this IGFBP on longitudinal growth [205]. Serum IGFBP-6 levels are not correlated with relative height in children with CRF, suggesting that interactions between serum IGFBP-6 and skeletal growth, if present, are probably complex [215].

Therapeutic manipulations of the GH/IGF axis in CRF

GH therapy and its impact on serum levels of IGF/IGFBP

If longitudinal growth is stimulated by circulating IGF-I and inhibited by circulating IGFBPs, GH therapy, an effective growth-promoting strategy in CRF, should alter the serum profile of IGF-I and IGFBPs. Supraphysiological doses of GH induce a rapid and persistent increase in serum IGF-I and, to a lesser extent, IGF-II levels in children with CRF [217, 240–242] (Fig. 31). During GH treatment, levels of IGF-I and IGF-II correlate positively with the increment in longitudinal growth, suggesting a role for the IGFs in GH-induced catch-up growth [217]. Similarly, levels of 'free' or readily accessible IGF-I rise during GH therapy. GH therapy lowers serum levels of the inhibitory binding protein IGFBP-1 by approximately 50% (Fig. 31) in association with increased serum insulin levels, suggesting that insulin mediates the GH inhibition of IGFBP-1 levels. Levels of IGFBP-2 and -6 are unaffected by GH therapy; IGFBP-4 levels do not change after 3 months of GH [205], but increase slightly after 12 months of therapy [218]. The levels of IGFBP-3, -5 and ALS, all components of the 150 kDa ternary complex, rise with GH treatment and show significant positive correlations with the increment in height [217]. The GH-induced increase in serum IGFBP-3 is confined to the 150 kDa serum fractions [242]. This suggests a role of the ternary complex in GH-induced catch-up growth. IGFs in the ternary complex are probably released by proteolysis of IGFBP-3. This lowers the affinity of IGFBP-3 for IGFs, allowing release of IGFs to proteins with higher affinity, such as IGFBPs in the 35 kDa

serum fractions and the type 1 IGF receptor on target tissues. These changes of the serum IGF/IGFBP profile lead to a threefold increase in the initially depressed IGF bioactivity into the normal range [240]. It is also possible that GH-induced increases in serum IGFBP-3 and -5 are accompanied by increased levels of these IGFBPs in extravascular fluids at target tissues, such as growth plate cartilage. Here, proteolysis of IGFBP-3 and -5 may stimulate growth by releasing bound IGFs in a process that does not involve ALS or the ternary complex.

In summary, GH exerts its stimulatory effect on longitudinal growth not by normalizing increased serum levels of inhibitory IGFBPs, but by increasing serum IGF levels. Some of the GH-induced IGF is bound in new serum ternary complexes, but the majority of stimulated IGF circulates in

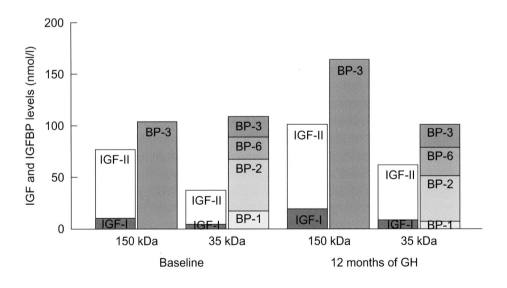

Fig. 31. *Balance between IGFBPs and IGFs in serum of CRF children before (baseline) and after 12 months of GH treatment. Levels of IGF-I, IGF-II, IGFBP-1, IGFBP-2, IGFBP-3 and IGFBP-6 in the 150 kDa and 35 kDa fractions of CRF serum are presented.*

Adapted from [242] with permission.

the 35 kDa serum fractions bound to previously unsaturated excess IGFBPs. This GH-induced rise in levels of IGFs relative to IGFBPs in the 35 kDa fractions of CRF serum presumably leads to an increase of IGFs in extravascular fluids, from where circulating IGFs have access to their target tissues (i.e. the growth plate) and are able to interact with the type 1 IGF receptor to stimulate longitudinal growth.

IGF-I therapy alone and in combination with GH

Theoretically, IGF-I would be a more specific therapy than GH for uremic growth failure, because it would compensate for the relative IGF deficiency in the uremic state. Studies in experimental uremia in the 5/6 nephrectomy rat model show that the

growth response after IGF-I treatment is almost comparable to that after GH therapy [243, 244]. Combined therapy with GH and IGF-I has an additive effect on longitudinal growth and anabolism in experimental uremia (Fig. 32) and has the advantage of preventing the hypoglycemia that occurs during IGF-I therapy alone [243, 244]. In addition to its effect on stature, IGF-I has direct anabolic effects and improves renal function. In normal subjects, IGF-I rapidly increases GFR and renal plasma flow by approximately 30% [245]. In adult patients with ESRD, IGF-I induced a sustained increase in renal function over the observation period of 4 weeks (clearances comparable to those generally achieved by dialysis) [246]. An intermittent treatment regimen (4 days on treatment, 3 days off

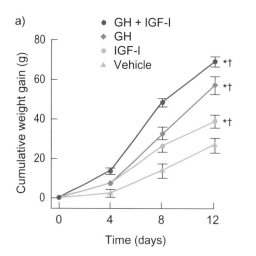
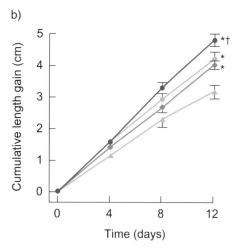

Fig. 32. Effect of combined treatment for 12 days with maximally effective doses of GH and IGF-I on weight gain and length gain in uremic rats. Both 10 IU GH/kg per day and 4 mg IGF-I/kg per day increased mean cumulative (a) weight gain and (b) length gain compared with vehicle controls. Co-administration of both hormones increased weight gain and length gain more than each single hormone. The effect was nearly additive when the growth-stimulating effects were analysed above baseline. Data are given as mean ± SEM. *Significant versus vehicle; †significant versus the other treatment modalities.

Adapted from [244] with permission.

treatment) for IGF-I (50 µg/kg per day) appears to be necessary to be well tolerated and to induce a sustained improvement of renal function. However, clinical studies with IGF-I have not been performed in children other than patients with GH insensitivity syndrome. The current limited interest by pharmaceutical companies and the lack of availability of clinical-grade IGF-I makes IGF-I treatment studies in children with CRF unlikely.

IGF displacers

The concept of activating the IGF axis, or increasing endogenous IGF-I bioactivity, has been proposed as a potential treatment modality. The idea is that by displacing bound IGF-I from IGFBPs, the levels of 'free' IGF-I should increase and thereby activate IGF receptors. Two independent studies [247, 248] have confirmed this hypothesis with the use of two different IGF-I analogs (Leu^{24,59,60},Ala^{31}hIGF-I and Leu^{24},Ala^{31}hIGF-I), which bind with high affinity to the IGFBP but do not directly activate the IGF receptor. One study showed that the administration of a 'receptor inactive' IGF displacer in the rat increased body weight, increased kidney weight and decreased creatinine and blood urea nitrogen, even though total rat IGF-I levels fell dramatically [248]. In an extension of this work, phage display has been used to discover synthetic peptides that bind to IGFBP [248]. In renal failure, in which free IGF bioactivity is low as a result of elevated IGFBP levels, the administration of IGF displacer peptides seems to be a logical way of increasing the bioavailability of IGF-I [249]. This is a more physiologic approach to manipulating the GH/IGF axis in renal failure and should have fewer side-effects than the administration of GH or IGF-I. Unfortunately, these peptides do not bind to rodent IGFBP, so their efficacy in animals is difficult to establish. However, because renal failure is characterized by excess IGFBP and not a deficiency of IGF, the concept of IGF displacement as a treatment option in renal failure seems promising. The concept of IGF displacement has been proved in animals, so a drug candidate with the desired characteristics is now needed in order to test efficacy in humans with renal disease.

Conclusions

Disturbances of the somatotropic hormone axis play an important pathogenic role in growth retardation and catabolism in children with CRF. A simplified overview of the derangements of the somatotropic hormone axis is given in Fig. 33. Whereas the GH secretion rate in CRF is variable between patients and studies, a prolonged half-life of GH as a result of a reduced renal metabolic clearance rate is a consistent finding. Accordingly, the serum GH levels in children with CRF are normal or elevated depending on the extent of renal failure. The apparent discrepancy between normal or elevated GH levels and diminished longitudinal growth in CRF has led to the concept of GH insensitivity, which is caused by multiple alterations in the distal components of the somatotropic hormone axis. Serum levels of IGF-I and IGF-II are normal in preterminal CRF, while in ESRD, IGF-I levels are slightly decreased and IGF-II levels slightly increased. In view of the prevailing elevated GH levels in ESRD, these serum IGF-I levels appear as inadequately low. Indeed, there is both clinical and experimental evidence for decreased hepatic production of IGF-I in CRF. This hepatic insensitivity

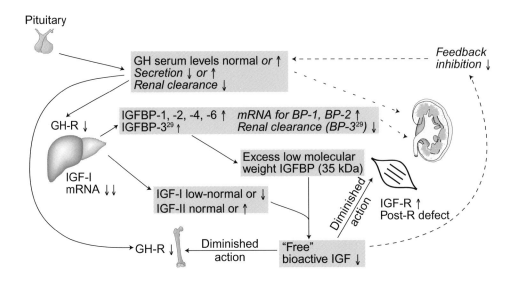

Fig. 33. *Current concept of the derangements of the somatotropic hormone axis in children with CRF. R, receptor.*

to the action of GH may be partly the consequence of reduced GH receptor expression in liver tissue and partly a consequence of disturbed GH receptor signaling. The action and metabolism of IGFs are modulated by specific high-affinity IGFBPs. CRF serum has a seven- to tenfold increased IGF-binding capacity that leads to decreased IGF bioactivity of CRF serum despite normal total IGF levels. Serum levels of intact IGFBP-1, -2, -4, -6 and low molecular weight fragments of IGFBP-3 are elevated in CRF serum in relation to the degree of renal dysfunction, whereas serum levels of intact IGFBP-3 are normal. Levels of immunoreactive IGFBP-5 are not altered in CRF serum, but the majority of IGFBP-5 is fragmented. Both decreased renal filtration and increased hepatic production of IGFBP-1 and -2 contribute to high levels of serum IGFBP. Experimental and clinical evidence suggests that these excessive high-affinity

IGFBPs in CRF serum inhibit IGF action on target tissues by competition with the type 1 IGF receptor for IGF binding. The relevance of the impact of alterations of the somatotropic hormone axis is underlined by the efficacy of GH therapy in growth-retarded children with CRF. The beneficial effect of GH therapy on longitudinal growth in children with CRF appears to be mediated partially by the stimulation of hepatic IGF synthesis, which results in an improved ratio of growth-stimulatory IGFs versus inhibitory IGFBPs in the circulation and, most likely, also at the growth plate.

Interactions between glucocorticoids and the GH/IGF axis

Long-term high-dose glucocorticoid medication in children inevitably leads to growth failure and protein catabolism. Recent evidence indicates that gluco-corticoids interfere with the integrity of the somatotropic hormone axis at various levels. However, the apparent discrepancies between *in vitro* and *in vivo* studies, short-term versus long-term exposure, and species-specific changes complicate a clear assessment of these interactions. A simplified overview of the impact of long-term glucocorticoid exposure on the somatotropic hormone axis is depicted in Fig. 34. The growth-depressing effects of glucocorticoids are certainly multifactorial and involve suppression of pituitary GH release by stimulating hypothalamic somatostatin tone, down-regulation of hepatic GH receptors, inhibition of IGF bioactivity by the induction of IGF inhibitors, complex alteration of the IGFBP serum profile, and a direct suppressive effect on local growth factor and tissue matrix production [250].

GH

There is a dual effect of glucocorticoid administration on spontaneous GH secretion *in vivo*. Acute administration of gluco-corticoids leads to a potent stimulation of GH secretion, indicating that glucocorticoids have a direct permissive effect on GH release at the level of the pituitary [251]. In contrast, chronic administration of steroids suppresses spontaneous GH secretion by increasing somatostatin synthesis (gene expression) and release at the level of the hypothalamus [252]. The threshold dose and duration of treatment required for inhibition of GH secretion under clinical conditions are not known.

GH receptor/GHBP

There is experimental evidence that long-term exposure to pharmacological doses of glucocorticoids suppresses GH receptor expression, at least in liver tissue.

Pharmacological treatment of uremic rats and healthy controls with methyl-prednisolone reduced the concentration of circulating GHBP, which is closely related to the GH receptor [188]. Hepatic GH receptor binding and liver-specific GH receptor mRNA transcripts in the rat were also markedly reduced in a dose-dependent fashion by dexamethasone treatment, which compromised the growth rate in these otherwise normal animals [253]. Under clinical conditions, GH receptor status can be assessed by measuring the high-affinity GHBP, which, in humans, is derived from the extracellular domain of the GH receptor by proteolytic cleavage. Circulating GHBP levels are significantly reduced in patients receiving glucocorticoids after renal transplantation [254]. Subcutaneous

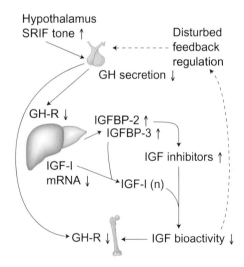

Fig. 34. *A simplified overview of the effects of long-term glucocorticoid treatment in pharmacological doses on the somatotropic hormone axis (SRIF, somatotropin release-inhibiting factor (somatostatin); GH-R, GH receptor; (n), normal levels).*

Adapted from [250] with permission.

GH treatment in these patients does not up-regulate the decreased plasma concentrations of GHBP. These clinical data confirm the experimental concept that long-term exposure to glucocorticoids reduces the sensitivity of tissues to GH by down-regulating the GH receptor.

The IGF/IGFBP system

If chronic glucocorticoid treatment suppresses spontaneous GH secretion, one would expect a decrease in concentration of circulating IGF-I, which is mainly regulated by circulating GH and nutritional status. However, the total concentration of IGF in children with Cushing's syndrome is similar to that of age-matched controls, although the growth rate of these patients is severely depressed [255]. Similarly, concentrations of circulating immunoreactive IGF-I in glucocorticoid-treated children with renal transplants were within the normal range [256]. These and other studies indicate that the stunted growth associated with hypercortisolism cannot be simply attributed to IGF deficiency. Rather, glucocorticoids antagonize the action of IGF by a direct and/or indirect mechanism, possibly by the induction of IGF inhibitors. These IGF inhibitors, which have a molecular weight of 12–20 kDa, differ from IGFBPs in several ways, but have not yet been characterized.

The action and metabolism of IGFs are modulated by specific high-affinity IGFBPs, which bind about 99% of circulating IGF. In one study in children with renal transplants receiving long-term glucocorticoid therapy, serum IGF-I and IGF-II were in the normal range; however, IGF bioactivity was significantly suppressed [256]. Immunoreactive IGFBP-3 was moderately elevated by 2.3 SD. GH therapy

led to a rapid and persistent increase in IGF-I concentrations, whereas IGFBP-3 concentrations increased only slightly. IGF-II concentrations did not change significantly. This improved ratio of IGF-I to IGFBP-3 led to a normalization of serum IGF bioactivity, which paralleled the marked growth stimulation in these children (Fig. 35) [256]. Chronic endogenous glucocorticoid excess in patients with Cushing's syndrome is associated with a slightly greater increase in IGFBP-3 than in IGF-I concentrations, normal IGFBP-1 concentrations and clearly elevated IGFBP-2 concentrations [257]. The molecular weight forms of IGF-I and IGFBP-3 in serum from patients with Cushing's disease did not differ from those

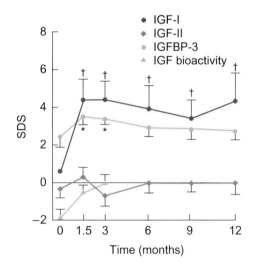

Fig. 35. *Serum concentrations of IGF-I, IGF-II and IGFBP-3 and IGF bioactivity expressed as SDS in ten children with renal transplants before and during 12 months of treatment with GH. GH treatment markedly increased IGF-I serum concentrations and normalized IGF bioactivity.*
* p < 0.05; †p < 0.005.
Adapted from [256] with permission.

seen in normal serum. Therefore, this study suggests a possible role for IGFBP-2 as an IGF inhibitor during long-term glucocorticoid excess.

Local effects of glucocorticoids

Glucocorticoids also interfere locally with chondrocyte growth and endochondral bone formation in various ways. They have been shown to inhibit the sulfation of cartilage matrix as well as the mineralization and formation of new bone [258]. In a cartilage model of cultured epiphyseal chondrocytes, dexamethasone decreased DNA synthesis and cell proliferation in a dose- and time-dependent manner by reducing GH receptor expression and inhibiting homologous up-regulation of GH and IGF-I receptors. Furthermore, glucocorticoids significantly lowered paracrine IGF-I secretion. These *in vitro* effects could be counterbalanced, at least in part, by the addition of GH in supraphysiologic doses to the cell culture medium [259]. It is noteworthy that other growth factors, such as calciotropic hormones, also strongly influence epiphyseal cell growth and exhibit numerous interactions with both the somatotropic hormone axis and glucocorticoids [88].

Reversal of the catabolic effects of glucocorticoids by GH therapy

Experimental and clinical data indicate that the catabolic and growth-depressing effects of glucocorticoids can be counterbalanced by concomitant anabolic treatment with GH. From clinical studies, two rationales for GH therapy of glucocorticoid-induced growth failure and catabolism can be given:

- in individuals with GH hyposecretion, GH treatment can be considered as substitution therapy

- in individuals who secrete normal amounts of GH but who have decreased concentrations of biologically available IGFs, GH is able to restore IGF bioactivity [256].

In experimental animals, GH was able to compensate for the growth-depressing effects of methylprednisolone [260] and, in a study in 32 healthy adult volunteers, GH was able to prevent the protein catabolic side-effects of prednisone [261]. These anabolic effects were also observed in subjects receiving long-term treatment with one-quarter of the dose of glucocorticoids and one-eighth of the dose of GH [262]. On the basis of kinetic data for leucine, the negative protein balance seen during prednisone treatment was due to increased proteolysis, whereas GH had no effect on proteolysis but increased whole-body protein synthesis. As prednisone and GH had different effects on fuel metabolism and insulin antagonism, GH and prednisone may reciprocally regulate the oxidation of protein and fat, while decreasing the efficiency of glucose disposal.

In summary, GH therapy antagonizes several of the side-effects of long-term glucocorticoid administration, such as growth failure, protein catabolism, and osteoporosis. In some studies, these benefits were obtained at the cost of increased concentrations of circulating insulin and glucose, indicating increased insulin resistance.

4.4 Thyroid hormone axis
Clinical findings

The thyroid hormone axis plays an important role in the regulation of tissue metabolism. Throughout childhood, thyroid hormone is involved in growth and skeletal maturation, stimulating both cartilage proliferation and epiphyseal differentiation.

Epidemiological data on the incidence of thyroid disorders in children with CRF are not available. In adults, the incidence of goiter shows a marked geographical variation [263], suggesting that environmental factors may be more important than CRF *per se*. However, the prevalence of goiter in patients with ESRD is increased compared with patients with non-renal disease [264, 265]. The prevalence of hypothyroidism ranges between 0% and 9.5% in adults with ESRD [264]. Primary hypothyroidism was observed 2.5 times more frequently in dialysis patients than in patients with other chronic non-renal disease; the prevalence of hyperthyroidism was not different [264]. In children, the prevalence of hypothyroidism may be higher due to the greater proportion of patients treated for cystinosis and nephrotic syndrome. In cystinotic patients, deposition of cystine crystals in the thyroid can lead to destruction of the gland and frank hypothyroidism [266]. Children with severe nephrotic syndrome, particularly with the congenital form [267], may become hypothyroidal due to the renal loss of thyroid hormone-binding globulin (TBG).

As some manifestations of hypothyroidism, such as hypothermia, pallor and dry skin, also occur in uremia, the exclusion of the diagnosis of hypothyroidism on clinical grounds may be difficult in a uremic child. Therefore, exploration of the hormonal status of a patient is essential for the recognition of an accompanying thyroidal disorder.

Iodine

Inorganic iodine is physiologically excreted by the kidney, and plasma inorganic iodine levels increase as kidney function decreases [268]. Basal radioiodine uptake by the thyroid is reduced in CRF [269]; this may result from an expanded iodine pool. In uremic rats, a direct correlation between thyroid gland volume and serum iodine levels suggests a pathogenetic role for iodine in goiter formation [270].

Thyroid hormones

The plasma levels of total T_4 and T_3 are decreased in patients with CRF [263]. Significant depression of T_4 and T_3 levels usually occurs once the GFR falls below 50%. Thyroid hormone production rates are normal in patients with CRF [271, 272]. Metabolic clearance rates of the hormones may [273] or may not [272] be increased. Due to impaired peripheral deiodination of T_4 to T_3 [100, 273], there is a more distinct suppression of T_3 than of T_4 levels. Diminished T_4 levels are found in a third, and diminished T_3 levels in half, of the patients with ESRD [265, 269, 274–277] including children [278]. Concentrations of reverse T_3 (rT_3), the inactive metabolite of T_4 in plasma, are low [279] or normal [276, 277]. Production and metabolic clearance rates of rT_3 are normal [271], but extravascular binding of rT_3 is increased [272].

The more pronounced decrease in plasma T_3 compared with T_4 levels in CRF resembles the thyroid hormone pattern observed in other states of chronic non-thyroidal diseases ('sick euthyroid' or 'low T_3' syndrome). However, whereas in the sick euthyroid syndrome, rT_3 levels are elevated as a result of impaired peripheral conversion of T_4 to T_3, rT_3 levels are in the low-normal range in CRF. This constellation has been explained by a redistribution of rT_3 into extravascular compartments in uremia [272]. The endocrine profiles of primary

Table 4. Abnormalities of endocrine status in CRF compared with primary hypothyroidism and 'sick euthyroid syndrome' observed in states of chronic, non-thyroid disease.

	Primary hypothyroidism	CRF	'Sick euthyroid' syndrome
Total T_3	↓	↓	↓
Total T_4	↓	(↓)	(↓)
Free T_3	↓	↓	↓
Free T_4	↓	↓	↓
Reverse T_3	↓	↔ or ↓	↑
TBG	↔	CPD/nephrosis: ↓ HD: ↔	↔
TSH	↑	↔	↔
TRH test	↑	↔ or ↓	↔

CPD, chronic peritoneal dialysis; HD, hemodialysis.

Adapted from Schaefer et al. Endocrine disorders. In Cameron et al. (eds): Oxford Textbook of Clinical Nephrology, 2nd edn. Oxford Medical Publications; 1997. p. 1854–66 with permission.

hypothyroidism, sick euthyroid syndrome and uremia are differentiated in Table 4.

Binding proteins

Circulating thyroid hormones are bound to TBG, albumin and prealbumin. TBG levels are usually normal in hemodialysis [269, 280]; they are frequently low in continuous ambulatory peritoneal dialysis (CAPD) patients, who lose thyroid hormone-binding proteins via the dialysate [280, 281]. Patients with severe nephrotic syndrome may have markedly low plasma levels of TBG due to urinary protein loss. Only the unbound (free) T_4 and free T_3 fractions are biologically active. Plasma free T_4 and free T_3 as measured by radioimmunoassay are low [282], and dissociation constants for specific T_4 and T_3 binding [283] are normal.

Thyroid-stimulating hormone

Despite low plasma total and free T_4 and T_3 levels, concentrations of thyroid-stimulating hormone (TSH) are usually normal in adults [269, 282, 284] and children [278]. Only patients with congenital nephrotic syndrome [267] and nephropathic cystinosis show elevated TSH levels.

TSH is secreted in a pulsatile fashion. In patients with CRF the frequency of plasma TSH concentration peaks is increased, but peak amplitudes are reduced [285]. No predominant frequency of the TSH pulses is observed by time-series analysis, suggesting a loss of the periodicity of TSH release [285]. The erratic pattern of small, frequent hormone pulses is associated with a loss of the physiological diurnal rhythm characterized by an evening rise of TSH levels in children and adults [277, 278, 285].

Administration of thyrotropin-releasing hormone (TRH) elicits a delayed and blunted, but prolonged, increase in plasma TSH levels both in adults and children with CRF [100, 150, 283, 286]. The responsiveness to TRH is inversely related to the duration of renal impairment [287]. Children with nephropathic cystinosis are exceptional in that, even in advanced renal failure, they exibit an exaggerated TSH response to TRH stimulation. This reflects primary hypothyroidism due to destruction of the thyroid gland by deposition of cystine crystals [266].

The mechanism for the relative TRH insensitivity of the pituitary in non-cystinotic patients is not clear. Dopaminergic blockade by metoclopramide amplifies TSH release in euthyroid subjects, but no increase was found in uremic patients [288]. This observation argues against hyperactivity of dopaminergic inhibitory neurons in the pathogenesis of abnormal TSH reactivity. Experimental evidence suggests an increased sensitivity of the thyrotroph to feedback inhibition by thyroid hormones. In addition to an abnormal responsiveness of the thyrotroph, the altered pattern of spontaneous pulsatile TSH secretion [278, 285] suggests an additional dysregulation of hypothalamic TRH release.

In summary, CRF is associated with alterations of hormone secretion and clearance at multiple levels of the hypothalamo-pituitary-thyroid axis. These alterations are compatible with a resetting of the central thyrostat towards lower levels of circulating thyroid hormones. The lacking up-regulation of spontaneous TSH secretion, despite low thyroid hormone

levels, may be interpreted in two ways. One possibility is a pathological disability of the thyrotroph to respond to the physiological stimulus of low thyroid hormone concentrations. Alternatively, the reduced responsiveness of the hypothalamo-pituitary axis may be a 'physiological' down-regulation resulting from a reduced demand for thyroid hormone in the specific state of metabolism caused by uremia.

Thyroid hormone action

Patients with CRF usually appear clinically euthyroidal. Measurements of basal metabolic rate and rough clinical indices yield normal results [274, 289]. Experimental data on thyroid hormone actions at the tissue level are somewhat controversial. Although the T_3 content of uremic rat livers is decreased and the activities of certain thyroid hormone-dependent liver enzymes are low in uremic rats [290], hepatocyte mRNA concentrations of various T_3-dependent proteins are normal [291]. As thyroid hormones act directly at the transcriptional level [292], these findings seem to rule out any major tissue element of hepatic hypothyroidism. T_3 receptor expression is elevated in patients with CRF [293]; this may represent a compensatory mechanism to preserve tissue euthyroidism.

Although the efficacy of thyroid hormones appears to be conserved at the nuclear level, other actions are compromised. Patients with CRF show a marked resistance to thyroid hormones with regard to thermogenesis. Oxygen uptake is neither stimulated by administration of T_3 nor suppressed by its antagonist sodium ipodate [294] (Fig. 36). Leukocyte ouabain binding capacity and Na/K-ATPase, which are low in both CRF

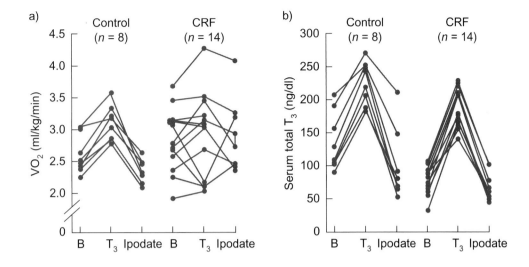

Fig. 36. *Changes in (a) oxygen consumption (VO$_2$) and (b) serum total T$_3$ in CRF patients and controls during T$_3$ and ipodate treatment relative to baseline (B). In CRF patients, administration of T$_3$ failed to stimulate and thyroid suppression failed to reduce VO$_2$, despite adequate changes in serum T$_3$ levels.*

Adapted from [294] with permission.

and hypothyroid subjects, are restored by thyroid hormone treatment in hypothyroid, but not in CRF, patients.

Nitrogen balance studies in uremic patients under T$_3$ supplementation show hypersensitivity to the catabolic effects of thyroid hormones [295]. The 'low T$_3$' syndrome of uremia may therefore be beneficial by reducing protein breakdown [279]. Similar phenomena are observed in patients with chronic illness or malnutrition [296].

On the basis of these observations, part of the changes to the thyroid axis in uremia may be interpreted as a physiological adaptation to conserve energy in an adverse metabolic environment. Supplementary thyroid hormone treatment might therefore not only have no beneficial effects but may even be harmful.

Diagnosis and clinical management of thyroid disorders in CRF

As the clinical features of uremia and hypothyroidism may be indistinguishable, all patients with ESRD should be screened for potential hypothyroidism. In a uremic patient, hypothyroidism should be diagnosed only if total and free T$_4$ levels are distinctly low, the TBG concentrations normal and the basal TSH levels elevated. A normal plasma concentration of TSH is probably a valid indicator of tissue euthyroidism. Treatment with thyroid hormones should be limited to patients with clinical hypothyroidism and elevated plasma TSH. The increased risk for induction of tissue catabolism by thyroid hormone treatment needs to be recognized.

In hemodialysis patients, heparin may interfere with the thyroid hormone status.

Heparin competes with T_4 at intra- and extravascular binding sites, thus increasing total and free levels of serum T_4 for at least 24 hours post-dialysis [297]. Therefore, strict standardization of the timing of investigations relative to dialysis is essential.

Patients with CRF who undergo repeated radiologic investigations with iodinated contrast agents may be at increased risk of developing iodine-induced hyperthyroidism because of reduced iodine clearance.

4.5 Adrenal hormone axis

Clinical findings

Analogous to thyroid disorders, dysfunction of the pituitary–adrenal axis may be difficult to diagnose in patients with CRF. Uremia shares certain clinical signs and symptoms with Cushing's syndrome, such as osteopenia, proximal muscle weakness with atrophy, glucose intolerance, negative nitrogen balance and hypertension [298]; therefore, Cushing's syndrome may be easily missed if it occurs concomitantly with renal failure. Similarly, adrenal insufficiency may present with symptoms that are not uncommon in renal failure, for example hypotension, weakness and hyperkalemia. To confirm or reject the diagnoses of Cushing's syndrome or adrenal failure, the clinician has to rely on evaluation of the patient's hormonal status under basal and stimulated conditions. For a comprehensive interpretation of the endocrine status, changes of the hypothalamo–pituitary–adrenal axis induced by CRF *per se* must be kept in mind.

Cortisol

Cortisol is conjugated in the liver to water-soluble metabolites, which are predominantly excreted by the kidney and accumulate in renal failure. While normal morning fasting cortisol levels are found in the majority of adult patients [299–302], the investigation of 24-hour profiles yielded clearly elevated integrated mean total and free cortisol levels [303].

The degree of renal dysfunction and/or the treatment modality may affect plasma cortisol levels. Whereas normal basal levels of plasma cortisol and no correlation between cortisol levels and GFR were found in children over a GFR range of 2–44 ml/min/1.73 m² [304], hypercortisolism was observed in 15 out of 26 children on hemodialysis [305]. The diurnal rhythm and the pulsatile mode of cortisol secretion is conserved in renal failure; however, the half-life of the endogenous secretory peaks is prolonged [299, 303, 306]. Elevated baseline concentrations may therefore either represent increased hormone secretion (e.g. due to an endocrine state of chronic stress) or be related to deficient clearance of the hormone from the circulation [307]. Compatible with the 'stress hypothesis', the secretory activity is increased in hemodialysis patients during dialysis sessions, whereas a normal pattern is observed on days off dialysis [303].

Stimulation of the zona fasciculata with exogenous adrenocorticotropic hormone (ACTH) in uremic patients yields a normal cortisol response, irrespective of whether supraphysiological [302, 305, 308–311] or low doses [310] of ACTH are used. Zona glomerulosa steroids (aldosterone, 18-OH-corticosterone) are stimulated normally in CAPD [300, 310] but not in hemodialysis patients [312]. Transient hyporesponsiveness to ACTH was observed in the majority of patients who returned to dialysis after transplant failure [313].

Adrenal androgens

Adrenarche marks an important milestone in endocrine maturation. Adrenarche occurs about 2 years before the initiation of puberty and is independent of it. Low plasma levels of dehydroepiandrosterone (DHEA) and DHEA-sulfate, the marker hormones of the zona reticularis, are observed in adult men as well as in pre- and midpubertal boys on hemodialysis, whereas normal levels are found in patients on conservative treatment [112, 314, 315]. Conversely, androstenedione, an adrenal androgen produced by the ACTH-dependent zona fasciculata, is elevated in patients on conservative treatment, and normal or elevated in hemodialysis patients [112, 305]. A similar elevation of androstenedione is observed in girls with CRF [126]. In renal allograft recipients, glucocorticoid treatment invariably lowers adrenal androgen production to almost undetectable levels [111, 112, 305].

ACTH

Basal ACTH levels are normal [302, 305, 316] or elevated [301, 308] in patients with CRF. The occasional finding of increased ACTH levels with normal cortisol levels has raised speculation that the bioactivity of ACTH may be reduced, but this has not been substantiated. The functional status of pituitary corticotrophs in uremia is still under discussion. ACTH secretion is not suppressible by standard oral doses of dexamethasone [308, 317]. Oral absorption of dexamethasone is, however, reduced in uremia [299], and suppression of ACTH can be achieved at higher doses of dexamethasone [299, 302, 303]. After intravenous administration of dexamethasone, only incomplete suppression of plasma cortisol levels is observed; however,

the metabolic clearance of dexamethasone is possibly increased in uremia [299, 318]. The responsiveness of the corticotroph to stimulation by metapirone may [308] or may not [299] be reduced in uremia. ACTH release after administration of corticotropin-releasing hormone (CRH) occurs early but is blunted [301, 316]. In normal subjects, acute hypoglycemia elicits a counter-regulatory stimulation of the CRH–ACTH–cortisol axis. In patients with CRF this stress reaction is markedly suppressed. The increase in ACTH and cortisol following insulin-induced hypoglycemia is blunted in patients on hemodialysis [299, 302], providing further evidence of disordered hypothalamo–pituitary regulation of the corticotropic axis in uremia.

Diagnosis and management of pituitary–adrenal disorders

The most frequent circumstance in which a nephrologist encounters adrenocortical failure is upon discontinuation of glucocorticoids in patients returning to dialysis after transplant failure. Also, accidental adrenectomies can occur during nephrectomies, particularly in young infants, and adrenal hemorrhage leading to functional disorders is not uncommon in the perinatal period in children with coagulation disorders and as a side-effect of therapeutic anticoagulation.

In addition, adrenal insufficiency is occasionally seen as a complication of amyloidosis, which also compromises renal function, as typically seen in patients with severe chronic vasculitis or familial Mediterranean fever. Demonstration of low cortisol levels and an insufficient cortisol response to ACTH is required to confirm the diagnosis.

In transplant recipients, adrenal responsiveness is suppressed by steroid treatment [313]. This poses the risk of acute adrenal insufficiency during severe stress, for example surgical procedures or after abrupt steroid withdrawal.

The diagnosis of Cushing's syndrome in a patient with CRF requires elevated plasma cortisol levels, measured by a radioimmunoassay in extracted serum. While a single measurement of cortisol may be misleading, loss of diurnal rhythm (24-hour cortisol profile) is a characteristic of Cushing's syndrome not seen in uremia-related adrenal dysfunction. Failure of high-dose dexamethasone, either orally (0.11 mg/kg) or intravenously (0.03 mg/kg), to suppress ACTH and cortisol levels is confirmatory evidence.

4.6 Hormones involved in carbohydrate metabolism

Glucose intolerance is a common feature of CRF. The introduction of the euglycemic and hyperglycemic clamp techniques has been important in understanding insulin and glucose metabolism in patients with CRF [319]. In the euglycemic insulin clamp technique, a given level of insulinemia is maintained, and blood glucose is kept constant by infusing glucose at a continuously adjusted rate. Thus, the infusion rate equals tissue glucose uptake and metabolism. This allows tissue sensitivity to insulin to be quantified. In the hyperglycemic clamp technique, blood glucose levels are acutely raised by a priming infusion of glucose, and then maintained at about twice the fasting level by a variable glucose infusion. Under these steady-state conditions, the glucose infusion rate is a measure of glucose uptake and metabolism by all cells of the body. The early plasma insulin response is an index of the β-cell responsiveness to the hyperglycemic stimulus, whereas the late insulin response is a measure of peripheral tissue sensitivity to insulin.

Insulin secretion

Fasting serum insulin levels are usually normal or slightly elevated in patients with CRF. In contrast, serum levels of proinsulin and C-peptide are elevated. This discrepancy is explained by differences in the relative contribution of the kidney to the metabolic clearance rates of the peptides [320].

In hyperglycemic clamp studies the early insulin response, an indicator of the pancreatic β-cell sensitivity to glucose, is variable: decreased [321], delayed [322], normal [323] or even increased [324, 325] responses have been reported. A decrease in initial insulin release in response to high glucose concentrations is found in isolated pancreatic islets of uremic rats [326]. The late insulin response is invariably increased in uremic patients, indicating tissue resistance to insulin, which improves on dialysis [327].

The variable β-cell response may explain why only some patients develop overt glucose intolerance despite constant peripheral insulin resistance. Glucose intolerance becomes manifest only when the β-cell insulin response to glucose is so impaired that it can no longer increase and overcome the peripheral insulin resistance [328].

Some evidence suggests a role for PTH in the deranged β-cell function of CRF. In children with CRF and severe secondary hyperparathyroidism, glucose intolerance resolves after parathyroidectomy, due to an improvement of the pancreatic insulin secretory capacity, whereas insulin insensitivity persists [329, 330]. High

PTH levels, with or without uremia, impair insulin secretion by a cAMP-independent mechanism [331]. Chronic hyperparathyroidism might enhance calcium entry into the pancreatic islets, resulting in an accumulation of calcium that impairs insulin release. This hypothesis is supported by the prevention of glucose intolerance and the normalization of islet insulin secretion in uremic rats treated with the calcium-channel blocker verapamil [332].

Tissue resistance to insulin

Euglycemic insulin clamp studies in adults [333] and children [334] with preterminal renal failure unanimously show marked decreases in tissue sensitivity to insulin, glucose uptake and metabolic clearance of insulin. After 10 weeks of dialysis treatment, all indices are markedly improved. The two major sites of carbohydrate metabolism are the liver and muscle. Impaired insulin action may be characterized by diminished visceral glucose extraction, increased hepatic gluconeogenesis, decreased peripheral glucose uptake or a combination of these. Most studies in uremic patients report normal basal and insulin- or glucose-suppressed hepatic glucose output [106, 333, 335]. However, these observations may be valid only for supraphysiological insulin concentrations. When endogenous insulin secretion is blocked by somatostatin and insulin is infused in physiological doses, suppression of hepatic gluconeogenesis is incomplete in uremic patients [336]. Moreover, isotope studies suggest reduced glucose oxidation to CO_2 and increased glucose recycling [335]. In contrast to these subtle changes of hepatic glucose turnover, glucose metabolism in the peripheral tissue is markedly impaired [333, 337, 338]. Hence, the major site of resistance to insulin-mediated glucose uptake in uremia is the peripheral tissue, mainly skeletal muscle.

In principle, insulin resistance may be due to changes at the membrane receptor level, the post-receptor level or a combination of these. Studies in adipocytes, monocytes, hepatocytes or human muscle tissue showed normal or even elevated density and binding affinities of the insulin receptor, and normal receptor-mediated transmembrane hexose transport [106, 339–344]. In uremic patients, glucose disposal was subnormal even after suppression of endogenous insulin secretion by somatostatin [345]. This observation suggests that the stimulation of glucose uptake by insulin is unchanged, but that insulin-independent glucose uptake is impaired. Thus, receptor expression and binding is normal or even increased, possibly as a result of homeostatic up-regulation in response to insulin resistance, and the stimulation of glucose uptake by insulin is intact.

Insulin membrane receptors are expressed in abundance, and maximal hormone action occurs when only 10% of receptors are occupied. Consequently, insulin resistance at the receptor level can be overcome by high insulin concentrations while a post-receptor defect cannot. Glucose uptake evaluated by the euglycemic clamp technique remains severely reduced in uremic patients even at the highest dose of insulin [106] (Fig. 11, p. 27). This observation is direct evidence of a post-receptor defect.

The exact step in the sequence of insulin-induced signaling events that accounts for the post-receptor defect is not yet known. In human muscle tissue, insulin receptor kinase activity is normal [344]. Insulin stimulates glycogen synthesis and glycolysis by increasing the activity of glycogen synthase (GS), phosphofructokinase (PFK), pyruvate kinase and pyruvate dehydrogenase. Glycogen levels are normal, and maximal GS activity is even elevated in muscle tissue of uremic patients [344], whereas PFK activity is diminished [346]. On the other hand, basal and stimulated lactate formation were normal or even increased in the erythrocytes of uremic patients, suggesting no impairment of glycolysis in this tissue [340]. Kalhan and co-workers demonstrated diminished glucose oxidation and increased recycling of glucose carbon in uremic patients, suggesting impaired glucose metabolism via the Krebs cycle [335].

Etiology of insulin resistance
Glucose intolerance in patients with CRF is partially corrected by dialysis [327, 347]. This observation suggests the presence of a dialyzable factor or factors in uremic serum that compromise the biological actions of insulin. Apart from dialysis, glucose metabolism is also improved by low-protein diets in children [348] and adults [349] with CRF. It has been hypothesized that low protein intake reduces the synthesis of a peptide inhibiting insulin action. Several peptides possibly interfering with glucose metabolism in uremia have been isolated [350–352]. Recent evidence suggests that $1,25(OH_2)D_3$ deficiency may play a role in the pathogenesis of insulin resistance in uremia [353]. Furthermore, insulin resistance improves in adolescents on dialysis after correction of anemia and amelioration of iron overload by recombinant EPO therapy [354].

Glucagon
Plasma levels of glucagon are markedly increased in uremia. This increase is in part due to cross-reactivity with the bioinactive 9 kDa proglucagon molecule [355]. The biologically active 3.5 kDa glucagon moiety is increased threefold. This increase is entirely due to decreased metabolic clearance; secretion is normal [356].

Glucagon exerts its hyperglycemic action primarily by stimulating hepatic gluconeogenesis. Patients with CRF exhibit reduced endogenous glucose output after a glucagon challenge [336]. Diminished glucagon binding with unchanged binding affinity by hepatic membranes was demonstrated in chronically uremic rats [357]. Normal basal, but diminished stimulated, adenylate cyclase activity was found. These results may be explained by receptor down-regulation in response to chronic glucagon excess, as healthy rats treated with exogenous glucagon exhibit similar changes.

The traditional view that glucagon acts only on hepatic gluconeogenesis may have to be modified because, in animals, chronic hyperglucagonemia causes impaired glucose tolerance [358]. Excessive glucagon levels also result in anorexia, ketosis and hypoaminoacidemia. The contribution of hyperglucagonemia to the catabolic state of uremia in humans remains to be elucidated.

Carbohydrate metabolism during peritoneal dialysis
Chronic peritoneal dialysis is characterized by continuous glucose absorption from the peritoneal fluid, which amounts to 2–3 g/kg/day in children on an average peritoneal dialysis regimen. In view of the known glucose intolerance of uremia, this

has raised some concern. Basal glucose and insulin levels are normal or increased in CAPD patients [322, 359–361]. A transient increase of plasma glucose and insulin levels occurs during a CAPD cycle, which is correlated with the glucose content of the dialysis fluid [359]. The area under the curve following an oral glucose load is increased in uremic patients on CAPD compared with non-dialyzed and hemodialyzed patients [340]. Conflicting results have been reported with respect to the effect of CAPD on glucose tolerance and gluco-regulatory hormones [339, 361]. Peripheral insulin sensitivity improves after initiation of CAPD [362]; the improvement is significantly better with peritoneal dialysis than with hemodialysis treatment [347]. Insulin binding affinity and receptor numbers decreased on adipocytes of CAPD patients

within the first 3 months of CAPD treatment, but no change in insulin sensitivity was observed as assessed by the effect of insulin on glucose uptake and lipogenesis [339].

The presently available information indicates that glucose intolerance is not exaggerated in patients on CAPD. Insulin resistance tends to improve after initiation of peritoneal dialysis, even more so than in newly hemodialyzed patients. This may be explained by removal of circulating inhibitors of insulin action. The observed decrease of membrane insulin binding capacity *in vitro* [339] may reflect receptor down-regulation due to chronic hyper-insulinemia. Whether the chronic hyper-insulinemia in CAPD patients has deleterious long-term effects is, as yet, unknown.

5 Growth plate disturbances

Summary

Growth plate abnormalities in both humans and mice with renal failure have been associated with abnormal expression of the parathyroid hormone-related peptide and/or its receptor. Little is known about alterations in the growth hormone (GH)/insulin-like growth factor (IGF) system at the level of the growth plate cartilage in chronic renal failure. Data suggest that growth failure in experimental uremia is due, at least in part, to a decrease in GH receptor density in the growth plate, and that this decrease may be overcome by combined GH/IGF-I therapy. The growth-suppressive effects of high-dose glucocorticoid therapy in childhood are mediated both by alterations to the somatotropic hormone axis, and by direct local effects on growth plate chondrocytes. The main molecular effect of glucocorticoids is the reduction of basal and hormone-stimulated IGF-I secretion, which is involved in cell proliferation. The growth-depressing effects of glucocorticoids can be compensated for by supraphysiological doses of GH or IGF-I.

5.1 Growth plate disturbances in CRF

Morphology

Longitudinal bone growth results from progressive replacement of growth plate cartilage by osseous tissue at the metaphyseal ends (endochondral ossification) and modeling–remodeling of previously synthesized bone. Physiologically, the rate and extent of growth for a given growth plate is determined by a combination of chondrocyte proliferation, matrix production and increased chondrocyte volume.

In experimental uremia in the rat, multiple abnormalities of the growth plate have been described, although the findings regarding the width of the growth plate have been inconsistent. Indeed, growth plate width has been described as increased, reduced or unaltered compared with rats with intact renal function [363–366]. Such divergent findings may be attributable to differences in the severity and duration of CRF and the methodology used. Cobo and co-workers, in their elegant studies in a model of advanced CRF, described how the strict coordination between the processes of cartilage enlargement, cartilage resorption and osseous tissue formation at the metaphyseal end is disturbed in CRF [363]. Cell proliferation, as assessed by bromodeoxyuridine labeling, did not differ between CRF and control rats, but both the production of cartilage and ossification were significantly slower in uremic rats. However, the two processes were differentially depressed in the sense that cartilage resorption/bone deposition was affected to a higher degree than cartilage formation. This led to a disequilibrium that resulted in an increased growth plate height as a result of accumulation of cartilage at the hypertrophic zone (Fig. 37). These changes were associated with an overall decrease in the expression of types II and X collagens, which was particularly marked in the abnormally extended zone of the hypertrophic cartilage [367]. Unlike collagen, the expression of collagenase-3 was not severely disturbed. Electron microscope analysis proved that changes in gene expression were coupled to alterations in mineralization as well as in the collagen fibril architecture at the hypertrophic cartilage. Because the composition and structure of the extracellular matrix have a critical role in regulating the behavior of the growth plate chondrocytes, these results are consistent with the hypothesis that alteration of collagen metabolism in these cells could be a key process underlying growth retardation in uremia [367].

The degree of secondary hyperparathyroidism may have an impact on the morphology of the growth plate in uremia. A reduced growth plate width and disorganization of the growth plate cartilage of uremic animals with severe

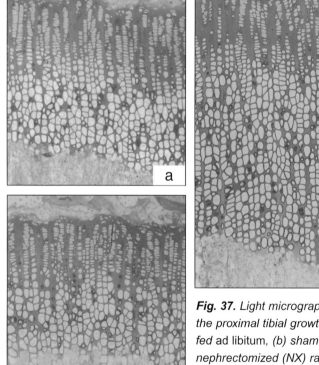

Fig. 37. Light micrographs of vertical semi-thin sections of the proximal tibial growth plate of (a) sham-operated rats fed ad libitum, (b) sham-operated rats pair-fed with nephrectomized (NX) rats, and (c) NX rats. The growth plate in NX rats appears larger than in either of the control groups.

Adapted from [363] with permission.

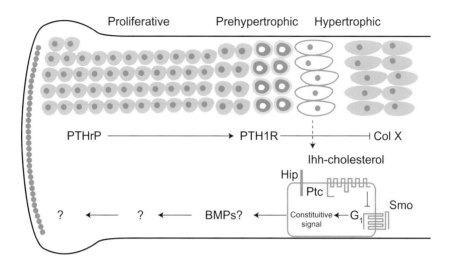

Fig. 38. *Regulation of chondrocyte proliferation and differentiation by PTHrP and Indian hedgehog (Ihh) (Hip, hedgehog-interacting protein; Ptc, patched; Smo, smoothened; BMPs, bone morphogenetic proteins; Col X, collagen type X).*

From [370] with permission.

secondary hyperparathyroidism have been described [368]. Calcium supplementation in uremic rats to induce biochemical changes consistent with adynamic bone resulted in impaired linear growth associated with marked widening of the growth plate, and disturbances in chondrocyte apoptosis, matrix degradation and angiogenesis [369]. Thus, both models of high- and low-turnover lesions are associated with growth retardation, but the growth plate abnormalities are markedly different.

PTH/PTH-related peptide receptor
PTH-related peptide (PTHrP), which frequently causes the humoral hypercalcemia of malignancy syndrome, is an autocrine/paracrine regulator of chondrocyte proliferation and differentiation that acts through the PTH/PTHrP receptor (PTH1R). PTHrP is generated in response to Indian hedgehog, which mediates its actions through

the membrane receptor patched, but interacts also with hedgehog-interacting protein (Fig. 38) [370]. Mice lacking PTHrP show accelerated chondrocyte differentiation, and thus premature ossification of those bones that are formed through an endochondral process [371], and similar but more severe abnormalities are observed in PTH1R-ablated animals [372]. The mirror image of these skeletal findings (i.e. a severe delay in chondrocyte differentiation and endochondral ossification) is observed in transgenic mice that overexpress PTHrP under the control of the α1(II) procollagen promoter [373]. Severe abnormalities in chondrocyte proliferation and differentiation are also observed in two genetic disorders in humans that are most likely caused by mutations in the PTH1R. Heterozygous PTH1R mutations that lead to constitutive activity were identified in Jansen metaphyseal chondrodysplasia [374], and homozygous or compound heterozygous mutations that lead to less active or completely inactive receptors were identified in patients with Blomstrand lethal chondrodysplasia [375]. Overall, these results underscore the pivotal role of the PTH/PTHrP receptor in the regulation of chondrocyte differentiation and bone elongation.

Disturbance in the expression of the PTH/PTHrP receptor have been reported in renal failure [376–379]. Gene expression of the PTH/PTHrP receptor is down-regulated in the kidneys of rats with moderate to severe renal failure [379]. Moreover, reduced expression of the PTH/PTHrP receptor has been reported in osteoblasts of adults with ESRD, particularly in those with low-turnover lesions of bone [380]. In the growth plate, substantial reductions in PTH/PTHrP receptor expression were also found in uremic animals with severe secondary hyperparathyroidism, and treatment with GH appears to modify the expression of the PTH/PTHrP receptor *in vivo* [368, 378]. Interestingly, these disturbances were not observed in nephrectomized rats with lesser degrees of secondary hyperparathyroidism or in those given calcium supplementation to induce adynamic bone [369]. Considering the crucial role of the PTH/PTHrP receptor in the regulation of endochondral bone growth, these findings suggest potential molecular mechanisms by which endo-chondral bone formation may be altered in renal failure, consequently leading to growth retardation.

In summary, based on the growth plate abnormalities observed in these human disorders and in mice with abnormal expression of either PTHrP or PTH1R, it appears plausible that impaired expression of PTHrP and/or its receptor contributes to the growth abnormalities in children with ESRD. Mild to moderate renal failure in animals leads to a reduction in PTH1R expression in growth plates and impaired growth, but it remains uncertain whether this contributes to altered chondrocyte growth and differentiation.

GH/IGF system

Little is known regarding alterations in the abundance and actions of the GH/IGF system at the level of the growth plate cartilage in CRF. There is decreased IGF-I gene expression, as demonstrated by *in-situ* hybridization and immunohistochemistry, in the growth plates of rats with CRF, and GH therapy increases IGF-I mRNA, particularly in proliferating chondrocytes [366]. Immunohistochemistry has shown that uremic rats have a decreased abundance of GH receptors in the proliferative zone, and only combined therapy with GH and IGF-I could overcome this decrease (Fig. 39) [381]. These data suggest that growth failure in experimental uremia is, at least in part, due to a decrease in GH receptor abundance in chondrocytes of the proliferative zone of the tibial growth plate. This decreased GH receptor abundance can be overcome by combined GH/IGF-I therapy, thus enhancing the generation and proliferation of hypertrophic-zone chondrocytes and increasing growth plate width. Metabolic acidosis might contribute to reduced growth factor expression in the growth plate, because murine mandibular condyles cultured in acidic medium exhibited less GH receptor, IGF-I and type 1 IGF receptor expression, and the expected increase in IGF-I mRNA expression with GH stimulation was inhibited in acidotic conditions [382].

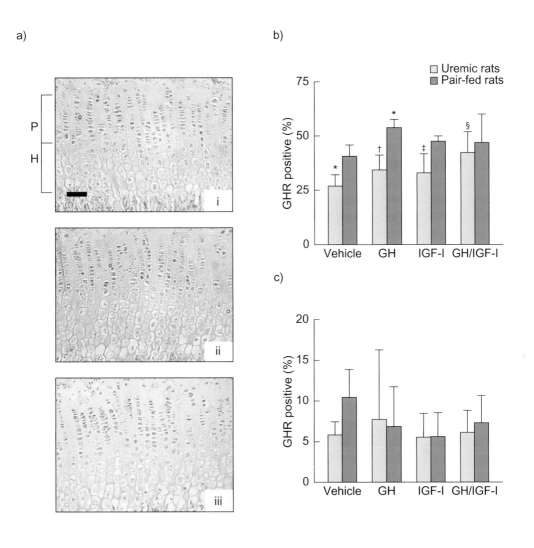

Fig. 39. *Growth hormone receptor (GHR) abundance in tibial epiphyseal growth plates is decreased in uremia, but increased by GH/IGF-I treatment. (a) Representative light-field views of immunohistochemical staining for GHRs (mAb 263) in tibial epiphyseal growth plates of (i) uremic and (ii) pair-fed vehicle-treated rats. GHR-positive cells are darkly stained. (iii) A tibial epiphyseal growth plate from a pair-fed vehicle-treated rat stained with MAb 7 control antibody. (P, proliferative zone; H, hypertrophic zone.) Bar = 50 μm. (b) GHR abundance in proliferative-zone chondrocytes. Data are expressed as the percentage of cells in the proliferative zone that were GHR positive. (c) GHR abundance in hypertrophic-zone chondrocytes. Data are mean ± SD.*
$p < 0.05$ versus vehicle-treated pair-fed rats; †p < 0.01 versus GH-treated pair-fed rats; ‡p < 0.05 versus IGF-I-treated pair-fed rats; §p < 0.001 versus vehicle-treated uremic rats.

Adapted from [381] with permission.

Impact of GH and calcitriol therapy on the growth plate in CRF

GH and calcitriol have potent and divergent effects on bone and mineral metabolism, but there is limited information on their potential interactions on chondrocyte proliferation and differentiation in renal failure. Dose-dependent inhibitory effects of calcitriol on chondrocyte proliferation have been shown *in vitro*, and neither GH nor IGF-I can overcome these inhibitory effects [383, 384]. *In vivo*, calcitriol doses ranging from 50 to 2000 ng/kg per day impair linear growth [385–387]. Moreover, Kainer and co-workers found that combined therapy with calcitriol and GH abolished the beneficial effects of GH on growth [388]. Calcitriol appears to attenuate the trophic effects of GH therapy on chondrocyte proliferation and differentiation as judged by reductions in thickness of the growth plate cartilage (Fig. 40). In addition, calcitriol appears to offset the GH-induced increases in type X collagen and type II collagen gene expression in animals with advanced secondary hyperparathyroidism [368]. Also, *in vitro* data indicate that the anti-proliferative actions of calcitriol in the growth plate contribute to the reductions in longitudinal bone growth observed during GH therapy in CRF. High and growth-inhibitory doses of calcitriol blocked the

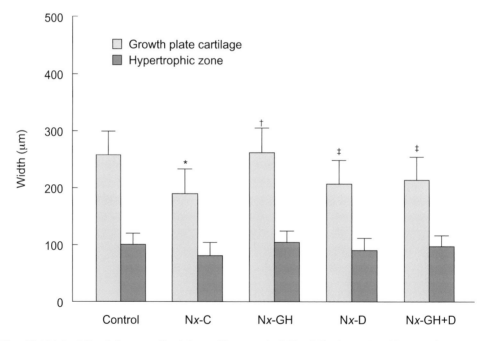

Fig. 40. Total width of the growth plate cartilage and width of the hypertrophic zone in rats with normal renal function (Control) and in four groups of subtotally nephrectomized rats with advanced secondary hyperparathyroidism. Nephrectomized animals received daily intraperitoneal injections of saline vehicle (Nx-C), GH (Nx-GH), calcitriol (Nx-D) or both together (Nx-GH + D) for 10 days.
*p < 0.001 versus control; †p < 0.001 versus Nx-C; ‡p < 0.005 versus Nx-GH.

Adapted from [368] with permission.

IGF-I-induced cell proliferation in an *in vitro* cell culture model [389]. These findings support the concept that calcitriol modifies the trophic actions of GH on bone and growth plate cartilage and that it can influence the process of endochondral bone formation.

5.2 Growth plate disturbances as a consequence of glucocorticoid therapy

Whereas normal glucocorticoid concentrations are permissive for skeletal growth, pharmacological long-term treatment leads to catabolism, osteoporosis, growth failure and even growth arrest. There are multiple mechanisms by which glucocorticoids exert their growth-inhibitory effects. The interference of glucocorticoids with the circulating components of the somatotropic hormone axis is described in Chapter 4 (page 52; *Interactions between glucocorticoids and the GH/IGF axis*). This section will describe the local effects of glucocorticoids in pharmacological doses on growth cartilage and the mechanisms involved.

Although changes in circulating GH, IGF-I and IGFBPs may, in part, be responsible for the negative effects of glucocorticoids on skeletal growth, the local effects appear to be even more important and at least partly independent of the changes in circulating hormones. This has been demonstrated impressively by the experiments of Baron and co-workers, who administered corticosteroids locally into the growth plate of the upper tibia of the rabbit [390]. After suppression of proliferation and growth, they observed catch-up growth following the withdrawal of glucocorticoids (Fig. 41). This catch-up growth was not mediated by circulating hormones, because the growth of the contralateral epiphysis was not altered, suggesting a mechanism for catch-up growth that is intrinsic to the growth plate.

Glucocorticoids inhibit the sulfation of cartilage matrix, mineralization and formation of new bone, and cell proliferation in the growth zone [391]. GH insensitivity was suspected to be one of the mechanisms. Controversial findings concerning regulation of the GH receptor by glucocorticoids have been reported. In rabbits, dexamethasone in growth-depressing doses caused a tissue-specific stimulation of GH receptor gene expression with a biphasic dose–response relationship [392]. In the rat, a reduction in GH receptor binding and in circulating GHBP levels in response to glucocorticoid therapy has been described [253]. Dexamethasone also down-regulates GH receptor expression of rat chondrocytes in culture, in association with suppression of cell proliferation [259]. In addition, there is an impairment of the GH-induced up-regulation of the GH receptor by dexamethasone, and an inhibition of the IGF-I-induced up-regulation of the type 1 IGF receptor [259]. Most importantly, dexamethasone inhibits paracrine IGF-I production and secretion into the cell culture medium (Fig. 42) [259, 393]. High-dose glucocorticoids also increase the rate of apoptosis in hypertrophic chondrocytes [394]. Both reduced proliferation and an increased rate of apoptosis are consistent with the reduced growth rate in *in vivo* studies.

In summary, growth depression as a side-effect of high-dose glucocorticoid therapy in childhood is partially mediated by alterations of the somatotropic hormone axis and partially by direct local effects on growth plate chondrocytes. In proliferative

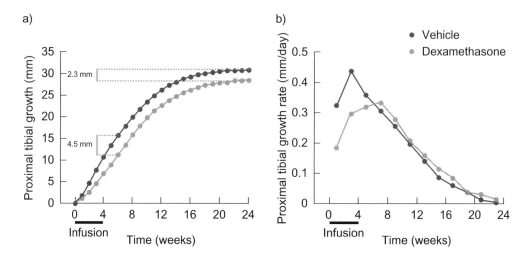

Fig. 41. (a) Cumulative proximal tibial growth during and after local dexamethasone infusion into the proximal tibial growth plate of 6-week-old rabbits. The bar below the x-axis represents the infusion period. The vertical bars at 6 and 24 weeks represent the difference in the cumulative growth between the dexamethasone- and vehicle-treated legs (each rabbit received both treatments). (b) Growth rates of dexamethasone- and vehicle-treated proximal tibiae. The growth rate was calculated from the proximal tibial growth over 2-week intervals.

From [390] with permission.

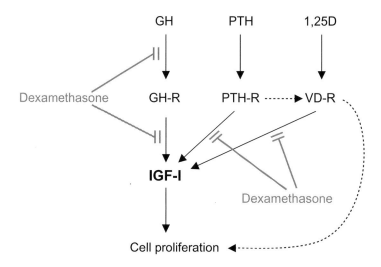

Fig. 42. Central role of IGF-I in cellular proliferation after stimulation with calciotropic and somatotropic hormones. (=, growth-inhibitory effect of dexamethasone; GH-R, GH receptor; PTH-R, PTH receptor; 1,25D, 1,25-dihydroxyvitamin D; VD-R, vitamin D receptor.)

Adapted from [393] with permission.

chondrocytes, GH and the calciotropic hormones PTH and $1,25(OH)_2D_3$ increase cell proliferation via stimulation of paracrine IGF-I secretion. Glucocorticoids decrease GH- and PTH- or $1,25(OH)_2D_3$-stimulated cell growth in a dose-dependent manner. Glucocorticoids in high doses reduce the expression of the GH receptor and type 1 IGF receptor. But the main antiproliferative molecular effect of glucocorticoids is the reduction in basal and hormone-stimulated IGF-I secretion. Results *in vitro* are in accordance with observations in animal experiments and in children treated with glucocorticoids, demonstrating that the growth-depressing effect of glucocorticoids can be compensated for by supra-physiological doses of GH or IGF-I.

6 Treatment of uremic growth failure

Summary

Growth hormone (GH) therapy should be started as early as possible in the course of renal disease in order to obtain optimal growth results. Growth in children with chronic renal failure (CRF) during early infancy may be improved by ensuring adequate nutritional intake, vitamin D supplementation, treatment of metabolic acidosis and avoidance of water and electrolyte disturbances. After infancy, however, these therapeutic approaches do not induce catch-up growth in short children with CRF. Although dialysis partially corrects the uremic state, it usually does not induce catch-up growth, and while a successful renal transplant restores the conditions for normal growth, growth rates after transplantation vary widely. Treatment with GH results in a sustained and significant improvement in height SDS compared with baseline values. Daily injections of GH have been shown to be the most effective dosage regimen. Started before puberty, the maximal increase in height occurs during the first 3 years of GH treatment, and final height is strongly correlated with the duration of GH treatment prior to puberty. Treatment should not, however, be stopped if height SDS gain becomes small after the third year of treatment or during the dip of growth velocity prior to the start of the pubertal growth spurt, as this may result in a further loss of height SDS. In general, children with renal allografts respond well to GH therapy started either before or during puberty. In renal allograft patients in whom alternate-day corticosteroid treatment does not induce catch-up growth, and discontinuation of medication is not an option, a therapeutic trial with GH may be considered. Irrespective of basal treatment modalities (conservative, dialysis, transplantation), the benefit of GH therapy for final height was 2.2 SD in boys and 1.7 SD in girls after an observation period of 8 years with a mean GH treatment duration of 5 years. Given its remarkable efficacy, GH treatment has relatively few side-effects in children with CRF.

6.1 General aspects

Adequate nutritional intake is the most important precondition for early infantile growth. Growth rates during this period are correlated with energy intake [61]. Consequently, forced feeding via a nasogastric tube or gastrostomy is an essential component in the management of infantile

CRF [395]. In later childhood, adequate nutrition is a permissive factor for growth; however, catch-up growth cannot be obtained by dietary manipulations alone.

Metabolic acidosis should be treated systematically [70] and water and electrolyte disturbances should be avoided [396]. Vitamin D treatment for the prevention of renal osteodystrophy is a further pre-condition for optimal growth rates. However, except during infancy, none of the above therapeutic procedures induces catch-up growth in short children with CRF.

Although dialysis treatment partially corrects the uremic state, early expectations of improved growth rates by dialysis treatment have not been confirmed. In a representative study in children on hemo-dialysis, about two-thirds of patients showed a gradual further loss in relative height. A mean of 0.4 height SD were lost per year [41]. Similar figures were reported by other centers [397, 398] and the EDTA Registry [399]. More intensified dialysis techniques, such as high-flux hemodialysis or hemofiltration, did not result in better growth rates.

The introduction of continuous peri-toneal dialysis was also disappointing with respect to the improvement of growth. Despite some evidence for better growth during short-term treatment [400], catch-up growth does not appear to be possible with this treatment modality. In patients on CAPD/continuous cycling peritoneal dialysis (CCPD) treatment for longer periods of time, a gradual decrease in height SDS is common [401–403]. As children treated with peritoneal dialysis are usually younger, the reported better growth rates on CAPD compared with hemodialysis may be due to a selection artifact. Even in infants starting CAPD/CCPD treatment during the first year of life, mean losses of between 0.7 and 1.3 height SDS during the first treatment year have been reported [25, 403, 404].

Successful renal transplantation restores the conditions for normal growth com-promised by the uremic state. However, growth rates after transplantation vary widely, from further deterioration of height SDS to complete catch-up growth [42–44, 405–410]. The main factors responsible for this variability are age, the immuno-suppressive regimen, renal function and the degree of growth retardation at the time of transplantation. The potential for post-transplant catch-up growth appears to be greater in young patients [411]. Infant transplant recipients exhibit excellent growth rates, with a relative height gain of 1.4 SD within 2–7 years [405, 412]. The degree of growth retardation positively predicts the post-transplant growth rate [413]. In contrast, pubertal growth seems to be least improved by transplantation. A recipient age greater than 12 years was identified as a negative predictor in a multivariate analysis [414].

Both the daily dose and the cumulative dose of corticosteroids seem to be inversely related to the post-transplant growth rate [2, 415–40]. A prospective randomized study in selected patients has demonstrated that an alternate-day corticosteroid treatment regimen is able to improve growth rates by 0.25–0.5 SD/year [408, 417]. The most impressive catch-up growth has been observed in patients in whom corticosteroid treatment was withdrawn [407, 418, 419]. In these patients, an improvement of 0.6–0.8 SD during the first post-transplant year was observed. However, withdrawal of corticosteroid treatment is associated with the risk of rejection episodes and deterioration of renal function in about 50% of patients [407, 420]. The hope that a prednisolone derivative, such as deflazacort, may influence growth less than conventional corticosteroids [421] has not yet been substantiated in controlled trials.

Post-transplant growth also depends on graft function [53, 413]. A marked deceleration in post-transplant growth is observed when GFR is below 60 ml/min/1.73 m^2 and, from the French experience, improvement of growth was observed only in children with a GFR above this value [44].

6.2 Treatment with GH

The GH resistance observed in uremia and during glucocorticoid treatment, outlined in Chapter 4 (page 34; *Disturbances of the IGF axis in CRF*, and page 52; *Interactions between glucocorticoids and the GH/IGF axis*), as well as studies in experimental animals which showed that the relative GH resistance can be overcome by supraphysiological doses of exogenous GH [365], has provided the rationale for GH treatment of children with CRF and after renal transplantation.

Prepubertal children
Several studies in prepubertal children with preterminal CRF have demonstrated an approximate twofold increase in mean height velocity (from 4 to 8 cm/year) in the first year of treatment with GH [241, 422–424]. This benefit was not attenuated by a strict low-protein/low-phosphate diet, prescribed in an attempt to slow the progression of renal disease [65]. A multicenter, randomized, double-blind, placebo-controlled study showed a growth rate of 10.7 versus 6.5 cm/year during the first year, and 7.8 versus 5.5 cm/year during

the second year in patients given GH and placebo, respectively [425]. The average increase in relative height was 1.6 SDS within 2 years, whereas the relative height decreased by 0.2 SDS in the placebo group (Fig. 43). The acceleration in growth was not associated with a disproportionate advancement of bone age.

Uncontrolled extended prospective studies over 5-year periods revealed the sustained efficacy of GH even after the second treatment year [4, 426, 427]. Although the maximal increase in height occurred in the first 3 treatment years, mean standardized height increased each year when compared with the previous year. A mean increase in height from –2.6 ± 0.8 SDS at baseline to –0.7 ± 0.9 SDS after 5 years was observed in American patients [426], an increase from –3.4 ± 0.4 to –1.9 ± 1.5 SDS was observed in German pre-

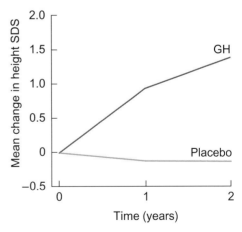

Fig. 43. *Efficacy of GH treatment in children with CRF. Mean cumulative change in relative height in children with preterminal CRF randomized to therapy with GH (n = 55) or placebo (n = 27). Growth improved only in the children receiving GH.*

Adapted from [425] with permission.

pubertal children [4], and an increase from –3.0 to –0.5 SDS in Dutch patients [427].

Prepubertal uremic children on dialysis, respond less well to GH than children with CRF on conservative treatment [220, 428]. While 38 children with a mean age of 6.5 years on conservative treatment gained 1.1 ± 0.8 height SDS within 1 year, the gain was only 0.5 ± 0.4 SDS in 18 dialyzed children with a mean age of 6.5 years [220]. The change of height SDS during the second treatment year was 0.5 ± 0.4 and 0.2 ± 0.4, respectively (Fig. 44). The French Society of Pediatric Nephrology has reported on 42 children on hemodialysis treated with GH [429]. Height SDS increased by 0.5 SD during the first treatment year. Growth velocity decreased over subsequent years, but remained higher than the pre-study velocity for up to 5 years. In the experience of the German Study Group, patients on hemodialysis and

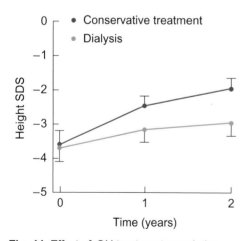

Fig. 44. *Effect of GH treatment on relative height in children with preterminal CRF receiving conservative treatment (n = 30) and in children on dialysis (n = 18). During the first and second treatment year the response to GH was higher in CRF patients prior to dialysis.*

patients on peritoneal dialysis did not respond differently to GH treatment [430].

In prepubertal children with nephro-pathic cystinosis on conservative treatment (mean age, 7.1 years), GH induced a mean increase in height of 0.8 SDS during the first treatment year and of 1.7 SDS within 5 treatment years [431] (Fig. 45). Again, children on dialysis treatment responded less well than children with predialytic CRF.

In pediatric renal allograft patients, in whom alternate-day corticosteroid treat-ment does not induce catch-up growth and discontinuation of corticosteroid medication is not considered an option for safety reasons, a therapeutic trial with GH may be considered. Several studies have dem-onstrated a marked growth-promoting effect of GH in prepubertal children with renal allografts over treatment periods of up to 3 years [432–437]. The median cumulative height increment was 1.5 SD during the first 3 years, similar to the effects observed in CRF patients on conservative treatment. In a large randomized study, growth velocity increased significantly during the first treatment year in the study group (7.7 cm/year) compared with the controls (4.6 cm/year). During the second year, growth velocity was 5.9 cm/year and during the third year 5.5 cm/year in the group receiving GH [437].

Pubertal children

A systematic analysis of the effect of GH treatment in pubertal children is difficult due to methodological problems [438]. These include delayed puberty with a lack of adequate reference values and frequent changes in treatment modality in this group. The factors that influence growth and the use of GH vary, depending on the type of

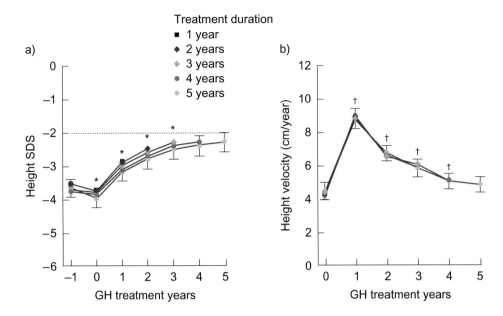

Fig. 45. *Effect of GH treatment in prepubertal children with nephropathic cystinosis receiving conservative treatment.*
*Significant difference versus previous year (p < 0.01); †Significant difference versus baseline (p < 0.05).

From [56] with permission.

treatment for renal disease. Whereas growth before and during dialysis treatment is affected by nutritional, metabolic and endocrine alterations, growth after renal transplantation is affected by glucocorticoid and other immunosuppressive therapy and graft failure. Among children treated with GH, treatment is usually discontinued after transplantation, but it is sometimes restarted if the growth rate remains low. This results in large variations in the duration of GH treatment, making assessment of its long-term efficacy difficult.

During the physiological deceleration of growth velocity in the late-prepubertal period, the GH response may appear disappointing and patients and physicians may consider stopping GH treatment. However, Hokken-Koelega and co-workers

have demonstrated that a sufficient pubertal growth spurt occurs if GH treatment is continued [427] (Fig. 46). The same authors also demonstrated that many transplanted pubertal children respond very well to GH when it is administered in the late-pubertal period [241]. The 2-year height gain was almost three times higher than in non-GH-treated historical 'controls' [439]. In the German study [3], patients were already treated prior to the start of puberty. Puberty was not advanced and no exaggerated loss in growth potential occurred during puberty. However, GH apparently did not exert a marked beneficial effect on pubertal height gain. It is important to note, however, that GH was continued throughout the pubertal period in only two-thirds of the patients, and the

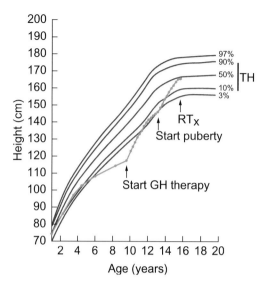

Fig. 46. *Individual growth chart of a girl treated with GH therapy for many years, showing a prepubertal dip in height velocity during the period just prior to the start of puberty. (RTx, renal transplant; TH, target height.)*

Adapted from [427] with permission.

fractional duration of GH therapy was positively correlated with total pubertal height gain.

Final height

Hokken-Koelega and co-workers [427] followed 45 children (prepubertal at start) with CRF for up to 8 years of GH treatment. Treatment resulted in a sustained and significant improvement in height SDS compared with baseline values. The mean height SDS reached the lower end (–2 SDS) of the normal growth chart after 3 years and even approached genetic target height after 6 years of therapy (Fig. 47). Table 5 summarizes the effects of GH on final height in various studies published until 2001.

Haffner and co-workers [3] followed 38 initially prepubertal children with CRF treated with GH until they reached their final adult height (Fig. 48). The patients were treated with GH during only 70% of the 8-year observation period, mainly due

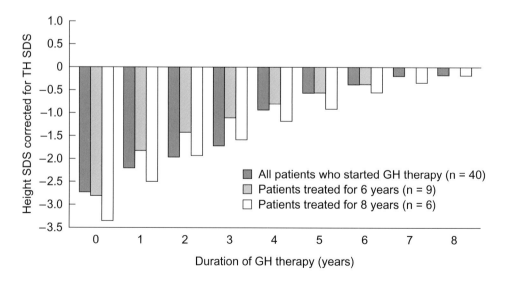

Fig. 47. *Mean height SDS corrected for target height SDS (TH SDS) during 8 years of GH therapy in patients with CRF.*

Adapted from [427] with permission.

Table 5. Synopsis of studies reporting adult height data after GH treatment of growth failure due to CRF.

Study	n	CRF treatment modalities	Age at start of GH (years)	Pubertal status at start of GH	Duration of follow-up (years)	Duration of GH (years)	Initial height SDS	Final height SDS	Change in height SDS
Dutch [427]	4	Cons. Rx/dialysis	< 11.0	Prepubertal	> 5.0	> 5.0	n.i.	−0.2*	n.i.
KIGS [440]	12	Cons. Rx/dialysis	11.9	Prepubertal	n.i.	5.0	n.i.	n.i.	+1.0
UK [441]	2	Cons. Rx	9.9*	Prepubertal	10.0*	0.4*	−2.2*	−1.1*	+1.1*
	5	Transplant	11.9	Prepubertal	> 6.0	2.9	−3.3	−3.0	+0.3
	6	Transplant	15.6	Pubertal	> 5.0	1.4	−3.4	−2.5	+0.9
NAPRTCS [442]	9	Cons. Rx	n.i.	n.i.	3.2	< 3.2	−3.0	−2.2	+0.7
	22	Dialysis	n.i.	n.i.	4.1	< 4.1	−3.6	−3.2	+0.4
	72	Transplant	n.i.	n.i.	3.7	< 3.7	−3.0	−2.5	+0.5
German [3]	38	47% cons. Rx, 24% dialysis, 29% transplant**	10.4	Prepubertal	7.6	5.3	−3.1	−1.6	+1.4
Belgian [443]	17	Transplant	n.i.	n.i.	n.i.	3.4	−3.0	−1.8	+1.2
Dutch [436]	18	Transplant	15.5	Pubertal	n.i.	n.i.	n.i.	n.i.	Total height gain 19 cm

Values are means unless indicated otherwise. * Median; ** percentage distribution of patient years spent in each treatment category.
Cons. RX, conservative treatment; KIGS, Pharmacia International Growth Database; NAPRTCS, North American Pediatric Renal Transplant Cooperative Study; n.i., no information given

From Haffner & Schaefer. Does recombinant growth hormone improve adult height in children with chronic renal failure? Semin Nephrol 2001;21:490–7 with permission.

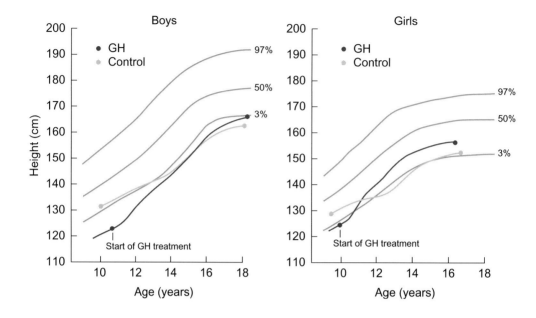

Fig. 48. Synchronized mean growth curves during GH treatment for 38 children (32 boys and 6 girls) with CRF compared, according to sex, with 50 control children with CRF not treated with GH. Normal values are indicated by the 3rd, 50th and 97th percentiles. The circles indicate the time of the first observation (the start of GH treatment in the treated children) and the end of the pubertal growth spurt.

Adapted from [3] with permission.

to renal transplantation, at which time GH treatment was stopped. Fifty children with CRF, matched for age and degree of CRF, who did not receive GH because growth was normal, served as controls.

The children treated with GH showed sustained catch-up growth, whereas the control children developed progressive growth failure (Fig. 49). The mean final adult height of the GH-treated children was 1.6 ± 1.2 SD below normal, which was 1.4 SD (1.5 for boys and 1.2 for girls) above their standardized height at baseline. In contrast, the final height of the untreated children decreased from baseline by a mean of 0.6 SD (0.7 for boys and 0.5 for girls). Calculating the increase in height SDS in

treated patients versus the loss of height SDS in untreated patients, the benefit of GH therapy was 2.2 SD for boys (i.e. 15 cm) and 1.7 SD for girls (i.e. 10.5 cm). The mean total prepubertal height gain was 18.6 cm in boys given GH, compared with 9.9 cm in the controls, whereas the total pubertal height gain was only slightly better in the GH-treated group (23.5 versus 21.0 cm) (Fig. 50). The latter finding may be explained, at least in part, by the fact that many children have not been treated with GH during the entire pubertal period because of renal transplantation. The total height gain was positively associated with the initial target-height deficit and the duration of GH therapy, and was negatively

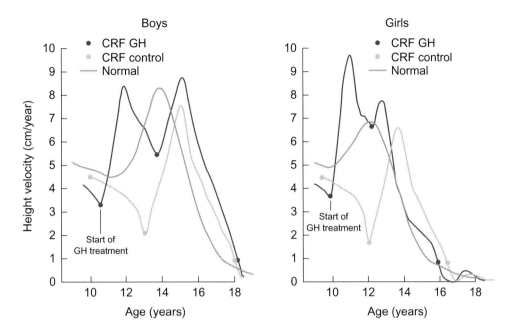

Fig. 49 *Synchronized mean height velocity curves during GH treatment for 38 children (32 boys and 6 girls) with CRF compared, according to sex, with 50 control children with CRF not treated with GH. The circles indicate the time of the first observation (the start of GH treatment in the treated children), the time of minimal pre-spurt height velocity, and the end of the pubertal growth spurt.*

Adapted from [3] with permission.

associated with the percentage of the observation period spent on dialysis treatment.

6.3 Strategies to optimize growth by GH treatment

The response to GH is influenced by age at the start of treatment (negative), GFR (positive), target height (positive), height SDS at the start of treatment (negative) and the duration of GH treatment (positive) [438]. A curvilinear dose–response relationship appears to exist. Although a dose of 4 IU/m^2 per day was more efficient than 2 IU/m^2 per day in a double-blind trial [445], no further improvement of the growth response was observed at a dose of 8 IU/m^2 per day, at least in a pubertal population [446]. Daily dosing is more efficacious than only three applications per week [447]. Discontinuation of GH treatment will result in loss of height SDS in 75% of children with CRF on conservative treatment [448]. In contrast, a percentile-parallel growth pattern is observed in most of the children in whom GH treatment was stopped because of renal transplantation [448]. Final height is strongly correlated with the duration of GH treatment prior to puberty [3].

In the light of these results, GH treatment should be started as early as possible in the course of renal disease to obtain optimal growth results (Fig. 51). The

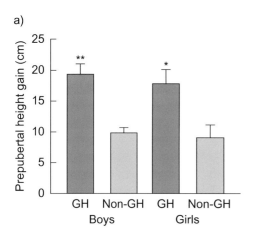

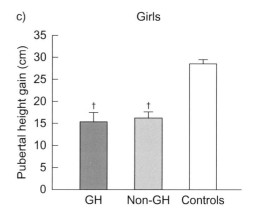

Fig. 50 (a) Prepubertal and (b and c) pubertal height gain in children with CRF followed from about 10 years of age to final height with or without GH treatment, and controls. Prepubertal height gain was measured from first observation until the start of the pubertal growth spurt. Pubertal height gain indicates the cumulative height gain during the pubertal growth spurt (same patients as in Figs 48 and 49).
*p < 0.01, **p < 0.001 significant difference versus non-GH; †p < 0.01 significant difference between CRF patients and control group

Adapted from [444] with permission.

dose of daily injected GH should be 4 IU/m^2 ($\equiv$ 12 mg/m^2 per day). Treatment should not be stopped if the gain in height SDS becomes small after the third treatment year or during the dip of growth velocity prior to the start of the pubertal growth spurt (Fig. 46). The duration of the pubertal growth period is significantly shortened in CRF patients, regardless of GH treatment, resulting in a markedly reduced pubertal height gain [3]. One might postulate that GH should be stopped at the onset of the pubertal growth spurt because no additional benefit of GH was observed. An alternative approach would be to continue GH at the standard dose of 30 IU/m^2 per week throughout puberty to make use of the possible additional potential suggested but not fully exploited in the German study. Finally, one might also argue that the dose of GH should be increased in puberty to mimic the physiological pubertal increase of endogenous GH secretion. Well-designed pros-

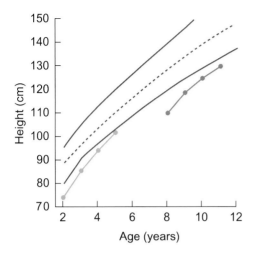

Fig. 51. *Age-dependent efficacy of GH treatment exemplified by individual growth curves predicted for two patients aged 2 and 8 years, started on GH at a basal height SDS of −3.5 and a height velocity SDS of −2.0. The broken line indicates the 50th percentile of a normal population, the solid lines denote the 3rd and 97th percentiles. Growth is accelerated over baseline height velocity in both patients by 4.5 cm in the first year, 1.9 cm in the second year, and 1.0 cm in the third year of treatment (empirical means of all patients on conservative treatment followed for 3 years). The young child reaches the 3rd percentile within 3 years, whereas the older child does not.*
From [4] with permission.

pective trials will be required to address the as yet open issue of GH continuation during puberty, which has important psychological, ethical and economic implications. At present, treatment should not be stopped until transplantation, to avoid the risk of catch-down growth.

It remains uncertain whether a low growth rate (height velocity below the 25th percentile over several years) should also be

a treatment criterion in a child whose actual height is still within the normal range. Such 'preventive' therapy might prove to be more effective in increasing adult height than initiation of treatment when short stature is already established. Such a treatment strategy seems in any case justified if growth arrest is noted. An as yet open question is whether, in very short late-prepubertal or early pubertal children, puberty can and should be postponed by GnRH analogs or aromatase inhibitors to prolong the prepubertal growth phase for GH treatment.

6.4 Adverse effects of GH treatment

Given its remarkable efficacy, GH treatment causes surprisingly few side-effects in children with CRF. A daily dose of GH of 12 mg/m^2 does not lead to accumulation (e.g. permanently elevated GH serum concentrations) [449], which might be suspected because of a reduced metabolic clearance rate of GH in CRF [176].

Concern was initially raised that prolonged GH treatment might induce diabetes mellitus, because patients with CRF already show impaired glucose tolerance due to peripheral insulin resistance. However, oral glucose tolerance remained unaltered both in children with CRF and in children after renal transplantation, when treated with GH for up to 5 years [66, 438, 450]. Insulin secretion, however, increased during the first treatment year and remained elevated thereafter. This increase was most pronounced in transplant recipients (Fig. 52). In children with nephropathic cystinosis who develop diabetes mellitus within the natural course of the disease [451], insulin secretory capacity becomes reduced before frank diabetes mellitus. As a

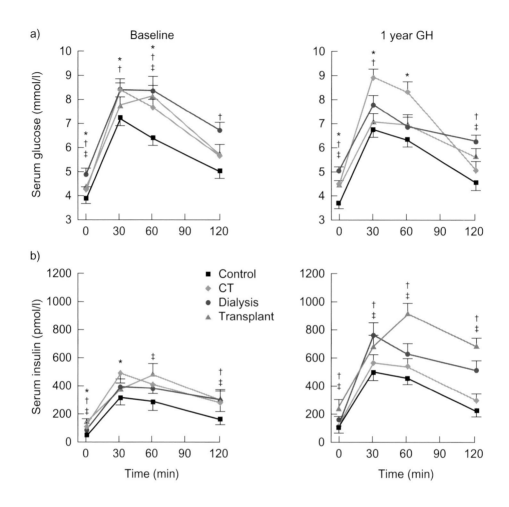

Fig. 52. *(a) Glucose response during an oral glucose tolerance test (oGTT) at baseline (left) and after 1 year of GH treatment (right) in CRF patients compared with controls (mean ± SEM). (b) Insulin responses during an oGTT at baseline (left) and after 1 year of GH treatment (right) in the same patients.CT, conservative treatment*
*CT versus controls (p < 0.05); †dialysis versus controls (p < 0.05); ‡transplant versus controls (p < 0.05) (ANOVA)

From [4] with permission.

consequence, the GH-induced rise in serum insulin levels was already lower in prepubertal cystinotic patients than in patients with CRF of the same age [431], and GH did not induce a rise in serum insulin concentration in many adolescents with nephropathic cystinosis after renal transplantation [452].

The long-term consequences of increased insulin secretion are uncertain.

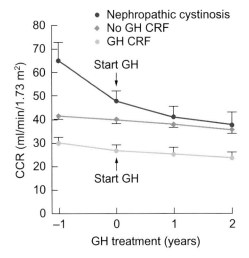

Fig. 53. *Effect of GH treatment on GFR measured as creatinine clearance (CCR). GH did not accelerate the loss of CCR in patients with CRF, nor in patients with nephropathic cystinosis. Data for control patients were taken from the European study on dietary intervention (65). Data are given as mean ± SEM.*

Adapted from [431] with permission.

Theoretically, it may contribute to atherosclerosis or induce diabetes mellitus by exhaustion of insulin-secreting β-cells. Although not a single case of irreversible diabetes mellitus has been observed in children with CRF [453, 454], a recent report of increased incidence of type-2 diabetes mellitus in children without renal insufficiency undergoing GH therapy requires prospective surveillance [455].

Slipped epiphyses [456, 457] and femoral head necrosis [458] have been reported as rare events during treatment with GH. Whether these complications were caused or intensified by GH cannot be stated with certainty, as both complications are noted with increased incidence in children

with CRF without GH treatment [91–93]. An aggravation of secondary hyperparathyroidism has been reported rarely [459, 460]. This seems not to be due to a direct stimulation of the parathyroid gland by GH, but might be an indirect consequence due to small decreases of ionized calcium as a consequence of GH-stimulated bone apposition or due to an increase in serum phosphate concentration. Furthermore, existing renal osteodystrophy may be unmasked by an increased growth rate and may become radiographically apparent [461].

Concern has also been raised that GH may cause glomerular hyperfiltration and accelerated deterioration of renal function. However, the physiologic acute increase of GFR induced by GH in healthy subjects is obliterated in patients with CRF [462]. So far, there is no evidence that GFR decreased more rapidly within an observation period of up to 8 years [3, 463]. A 5-year follow-up of GH-treated patients showed an average loss of no more than 8 ml/1.73 m² per minute [426]. Even in patients with nephropathic cystinosis, no acceleration of progressive renal failure could be substantiated (Fig. 53) [431].

GH is an immunomodulatory substance [464], which might trigger rejection episodes in patients with renal allografts. While a retrospective analysis [465] and several uncontrolled [256, 432–435] and controlled studies [436, 466] have not disclosed any effects on rejection activity, randomized prospective studies have provided some evidence for an increased incidence of acute rejection episodes. These, however, may be limited to high-risk patients who had experienced more than one rejection episode prior to the start of GH treatment [437, 467].

Contrary to concerns from 1987 [468], an extended survey of thousands of patients failed to reveal any significant relationship between GH treatment and leukemia [469, 470]. A review of adverse events in 583 patients with CRF and ESRD treated with GH, revealed one solid tumor and one β-cell lymphoma among patients undergoing peritoneal dialysis, and one β-cell lymphoma in a transplant recipient [471]. Recent reports on renal cell carcinoma, which developed in two patients, 9 and 11 years post-transplantation and who had received GH, and a case of chronic myelogenous leukemia in an 18-year-old GH-treated male with a failing cadaver donor transplant [472] raised the question of whether tumor risk may be increased by GH in post-transplant patients receiving long-term immunosuppression. The present data do not allow such a conclusion to be drawn [473].

Whereas benign intracranial hypertension has been reported as a rare adverse effect of GH-treated patients with various primary diseases, CRF appears to increase the risk of this complication by about tenfold [474, 475]. A recent survey noted symptoms or signs of intracranial hypertension with papillary edema during GH therapy in 15 cases out of approximately 1670 patients (0.9%) with renal disease [475]. All but two patients were symptomatic; the symptoms generally abated when GH therapy was discontinued, but two patients had persistent blindness. At least four of these patients had recurrence of intracranial hypertension after re-initiation of GH therapy. Many of the affected patients presented with predisposing conditions, but GH appeared to have been the precipitating factor.

The median duration of GH treatment before the onset of symptoms or signs was 13 weeks. It is therefore prudent to start GH treatment after a funduscopic examination by gradually increasing the dose from 50% to 100% of the maintenance dose within 1–2 months. As hypertension and fluid overload may be predisposing factors, both should be well controlled at the start of treatment. Headache, vomiting and other clinical signs of increased intracranial hypertension mandate a careful clinical investigation including funduscopy. The risk and benefit ratio must be carefully checked if a patient restarts GH treatment following the reversal of symptoms.

References

1. Cameron N. *The measurement of human growth*. London and Sydney: Croom Helm Ltd; 1984. p. 182.

2. Schaefer F, Seidel C, Binding A, Gasser T, Largo RH, Prader A, *et al*. Pubertal growth in chronic renal failure. *Pediatr Res* 1990;**28**:5–10.

3. Haffner D, Schaefer F, Nissel R, Wühl E, Tönshoff B, Mehls O, German Study Group for Growth Hormone Treatment in chronic renal failure. Effect of growth hormone treatment on adult height of children with chronic renal failure. *N Engl J Med* 2000;**343**:923–30.

4. Haffner D, Wühl E, Schaefer F, Nissel R, Tönshoff B, Mehls O. Factors predictive of the short- and long-term efficacy of growth hormone treatment in prepubertal children with chronic renal failure. German Study Group for Growth Hormone Treatment in Children with Chronic Renal Failure. *J Am Soc Nephrol* 1998;**9**:1899–907.

5. Rikken B, Wit JM. Prepubertal height velocity references over a wide age range. *Arch Dis Child* 1992;**67**:1277–80.

6. Marshall WA, Tanner JM. Variations in pattern of pubertal changes in girls. *Arch Dis Child* 1969;**44**:291–303.

7. Marshall WA, Tanner JM. Variations in the pattern of pubertal changes in boys. *Arch Dis Child* 1970;**45**:13–23.

8. Zachmann M, Prader A, Kind H, Häfliger H, Budliger H. Testicular volume during adolescence: cross-sectional and longitudinal studies. *Helv Paediatr Acta* 1974;**29**:61–72.

9. Cole TJ, Green PJ. Smoothing reference centile curves: the LMS method and penalized likelihood. *Stat Med* 1992;**11**:1305–19.

10. Schaefer F, Georgi M, Wühl E, Schärer K. Body mass index and percentage fat mass in healthy German schoolchildren and adolescents. *Int J Obes Relat Metab Disord* 1998;**22**:461–9.

11. Schaefer F, Wühl E, Feneberg R, Mehls O, Schärer K. Assessment of body composition in children with chronic renal failure. *Pediatr Nephrol* 2000;**14**:673–8.

12. Feneberg R, Bürkel E, Sahm K, Weck K, Mehls O, Schaefer F. Long term effects of tube feeding on growth and body composition in children. *Pediatr Nephrol* 1999;**13**:C78.

13. Schaefer F, Georgi M, Zieger A, Schärer K. Usefulness of bioelectric impedance and skinfold measurements in predicting fat-free mass derived from total body potassium in children. *Pediatr Res* 1994;**35**:617–24.

14. Slaughter MH, Lohman TG, Boileau RA, Horswill CA, Stillman RJ, van Loan MD, *et al*. Skinfold equations for estimation of body fatness in children and youth. *Hum Biol* 1988;**60**:709–23.

15. Houtkooper LB, Lohman TG, Going SB, Hall MC. Validity of bioelectrical impedance for body composition assessment in children. *J Appl Physiol* 1989;**66**:814–21.

16. Widdowson EM. Changes in body proportions and composition during growth. In: Davis JA; Dobbing J, editors. *Scientific foundations of Pediatrics*. London: William Heinemann Medical Books Ltd; 1974; p. 153–63.

17. Gregory JW, Greene SA, Scrimgeour CM, Rennie MJ. Body water measurement in growth disorders: a comparison of bioelectrical impedance and skinfold thickness techniques with isotope dilution. *Arch Dis Child* 1991;**66**:220–2.

18. Wühl E, Fusch C, Schärer K, Mehls O, Schaefer F. Assessment of total body water in paediatric patients on dialysis. *Nephrol Dial Transplant* 1996;**11**:75–80.

19. Wühl E, Wiens C, Daschner M, Fusch C, Schaefer F. Assessmemt of total and extracellular body water in pediatric dialysis patients by multifrequency bioelectrical impedance analysis. *Pediatr Nephrol* 1997;**11**:C27.

20. Aufricht C, Müller T, Lothaller MA, Kitzmüller E, Balzar E. Filling volume of peritoneal cavity does not influence measurement of total body water by bioelectrical impedance in children. *Perit Dial Int* 1995;**15**:171–4.

21. Schaefer F, Hake B, Schulte R, Schärer K. Changes of body composition in children following renal transplantation. *Pediatr Res* 1992;**31**:625A.

22. Jones RWA, Rigden SP, Barratt TM, Chantler C. The effects of chronic renal failure in infancy on growth, nutritional status and body composition. *Pediatr Res* 1982;**16**:784–91.

23. Kleinknecht C, Broyer M, Huot D, Marti-Henneberg C, Dartois A. Growth and development of nondialyzed children with chronic renal failure. *Kidney Int* 1983;**24**:40–7.

24. Rizzoni G, Basso T, Setari M. Growth in children with chronic renal failure on conservative treatment. *Kidney Int* 1984;**26**:52–8.

25. Warady BA, Kriley MA, Lovell H, Farrell SE, Hellerstein S. Growth and development of infants with end-stage renal disease receiving long-term peritoneal dialysis. *J Pediatr* 1988;**112**:714–19.

26. Rees L, Rigden SPA, Ward GM. Chronic renal failure and growth. *Arch Dis Child* 1989; **64**:573–7.

27. Karlberg J, Schaefer F, Hennicke M, Wingen AM, Rigden S, Mehls O. Early age-dependent

growth impairment in chronic renal failure. European Study Group for Nutritional Treatment of Chronic Renal Failure in Childhood. *Pediatr Nephrol* 1996;**10**:283–7.

28. Schaefer F, Wingen AM, Hennicke M, Rigden S, Mehls O. Growth charts for prepubertal children with chronic renal failure due to congenital renal disorders. European Study Group for Nutritional Treatment of Chronic Renal Failure in Childhood. *Pediatr Nephrol* 1996;**10**:288–93.

29. Schärer K, Chantler C, Brunner FP, Gurland HJ, Jacobs C, Selwood NH, *et al.* Combined report on regular dialysis and transplantation of children in Europe, 1975. *Proc Eur Dial Transplant Assoc* 1976;**13**:3–103.

30. Schärer K. Study on pubertal development in chronic renal failure. Growth and development of children with chronic renal failure. *Acta Paediatr Scand Suppl* 1990;**366**:90–2.

31. Rizzoni G, Broyer M, Brunner FP, Brynger H, Challah S, Kramer P, *et al.* Combined report on regular dialysis and transplantation of children in Europe, XIII, 1983. *Proc Eur Dial Transplant Assoc Eur Ren Assoc* 1985;**21**:66–95.

32. Schärer K. *Growth and endocrine changes in children with chronic renal failure.* Basel: Karger; 1989.

33. Ehrich JHH, Rizzoni G, Brunner FP, Brynger H, Geerlings W, Fassbinder W, et al. Combined report on regular dialysis and transplantation in Europe, 1989. *Nephrol Dial Transplant* 1991; **6**(Suppl):37–47.

34. Largo RH, Prader A. Pubertal development in Swiss girls. *Helv Paediatr Acta* 1983;**38**:229–343.

35. Burke BA, Lindgren B, Wick M, Holley K, Manivel C. Testicular germ cell loss in children with renal failure. *Pediatr Pathol* 1989;**9**:433–44.

36. Schaefer F, Walther U, Ruder H, Huber W, Marr J, Schärer K. Reduced spermaturia in adolescent and young adult patients after renal transplantation (Tx). *Nephrol Dial Transplant* 1991;**6**:840.

37. Palmer BF. Sexual dysfunction in uremia. *J Am Soc Nephrol* 1999;**10**:1381–8.

38. Hou S. Pregnancy in chronic renal insufficiency and end-stage renal disease. *Am J Kidney Dis* 1999;**33**(2):235–52.

39. Chan WS, Okun N, Kjellstrand CM. Pregnancy in chronic dialysis: a review and analysis of the literature. *Int J Artif Organs* 1998;**21**(5):259–68.

40. Nakabayashi M, Adachi T, Itoh S, Kobayashi M, Mishina J, Nishida H. Perinatal and infant outcome of pregnant patients undergoing chronic hemodialysis. *Nephron* 1999;**82**(1):27–31.

41. Kleinknecht C, Broyer M, Gagnadoux M, Marti-Henneberg C, Dartois A, Kermanach C, *et al.* Growth in children treated with long-term dialysis. A study of 76 patients. *Adv Nephrol* 1980;**9**:133–66.

42. Offner G, Hoyer PF, Jüppner H, Krohn HP, Brodehl J. Somatic growth after kidney transplantation. *Am J Dis Child* 1987;**141**:541–6.

43. Rees L, Greene SA, Adlard P, Jones J, Haycock GB, Rigden SP, *et al.* Growth and endocrine function after renal transplantation. *Arch Dis Child* 1988;**63**:1326–32.

44. Broyer M, Guest G. Growth after kidney transplantation – a single centre experience. In: Schärer K, editor. *Growth and endocrine changes in children and adolescents with chronic renal failure.* Pediatric and Adolescent Endocrinology Vol. 20. Basel: Karger; 1989. p. 36–45.

45. Betts PR, White RHR. Growth potential and skeletal maturity in children with chronic renal insufficiency. *Nephron* 1976;**16**:325–32.

46. Cundall DB, Brocklebank JT, Buckler JMH. Which bone age in chronic renal insufficiency and end-stage renal disease? *Pediatr Nephrol* 1988;**2**:200–4.

47. van Steenbergen MW, Wit JM, Donckerwolcke RA. Testosterone esters advance skeletal maturation more than growth in short boys with chronic renal failure and delayed puberty. *Eur J Pediatr* 1991;**150**:676–780.

48. van Diemen-Steenvoorde R, Donckerwolcke RA, Brackel H, Wolff ED, de Jong MC. Growth and sexual maturation in children after kidney transplantation. *J Pediatr* 1987;**110**:351–6.

49. Grushkin CM, Fine RN. Growth in children following renal transplantation. *Am J Dis Child* 1973;**125**:514–16.

50. Rizzoni G, Broyer M, Brunner FP, Brynger H, Challah S, Fassbinder W, *et al.* Combined report on regular hemodialysis and transplantation in Europe, 1985. *Eur Dial Transplant Assoc* 1986;**23**:55–83.

51. Chantler C, Broyer M, Donckerwolcke RA, Brynger H, Brunner FP, Jacobs C, *et al.* Growth and rehabilitation of long-term survivors of treatment for end-stage renal failure in childhood. *Proc Eur Dial Transplant Assoc* 1981;**18**:329–39.

52. Gilli G, Mehls O, Schärer K. Final height of children with chronic renal failure. *Proc Eur Dial Transplant Assoc* 1984;**21**:830–6.

53. Fennell RS (III), Love JT, Carter RL, Hudson TM, Pfaff WW, Howard RJ, et al. Statistical analysis of statural growth following kidney transplantation. *Eur J Pediatr* 1986;**145**:377–9.

54. Schaefer F, Gilli G, Schärer K. Pubertal growth and final height in chronic renal failure. In: Schärer K, editor. *Growth and endocrine changes in children and adolescents with chronic renal failure.* Pediatric and Adolescent Endocrinology Vol. 22. Basel: Karger; 1989; p. 59–69.

55. Hokken-Koelega AC, Van Zaal MA, van Bergen W, de Ridder MA, Stijnen T, Wolff ED, et al. Final height and its predictive factors after renal transplantation in childhood. *Pediatr Res* 1994;**36**:323–8.

56. Wühl E, Haffner D, Offner G, Broyer M, van't Hoff WG, Mehls O. European Study Group on Growth Hormone Treatment in children with nephropathic cystinosis. Long-term treatment with growth hormone in short children with nephropathic cystinosis. *J Pediatr* 2001;**138**:880–7.

57. Orejas G, Santos F, Malaga S, Rey C, Cobo A, Simarro M. Nutritional status of children with moderate chronic renal failure. *Pediatr Nephrol* 1995;**9**:52–6.

58. Foreman JW, Abitbol CL, Trachtman H, Garin EH, Feld LG, Strife CF, *et al*. Nutritional intake in children with renal insufficiency: a report of the Growth Failure in Children with Renal Diseases Study. *J Am Coll Nutr* 1996;**15**:579–85.

59. Baur LA, Knight JF, Crawford BA, Reed E, Roy LP, Allen BJ, *et al*. Total body nitrogen in children with chronic renal failure and short stature. *Eur J Clin Nutr* 1994;**48**:433–41.

60. Mehls O, Ritz E, Gilli G, Bartholomé K, Beißbarth H, Hohenegger M, *et al*. Nitrogen metabolism and growth in experimental uremia. *Int J Pediatr Nephrol* 1980;**1**:34–41.

61. Arnold WC, Danford D, Holliday MA. Effects of calorie supplementation on growth in uremia. *Kidney Int* 1983;**24**:205–9.

62. Betts PR, Magrath G, White RHR. Role of dietary energy supplementation in growth of children with chronic renal insufficiency. *BMJ* 1977;**1**:416–18.

63. Lucas LM, Kumar KL, Smith DL. Gynecomastia: a worrisome problem for the patient. *Postgrad Med* 1987;**82**:73–81.

64. Jones R, Dalton RN, Turner C, Start K, Haycock GB, Chantler C. Oral essential aminoacid and ketoacid supplements in children with chronic renal failure. *Kidney Int* 1983;**24**:95–103.

65. Wingen AM, Fabian-Bach C, Schaefer F, Mehls O. Randomised multicentre study of a low-protein diet on the progression of chronic renal failure in children. European Study Group of Nutritional Treatment of Chronic Renal Failure in Childhood. *Lancet* 1997;**349**:1117–23.

66. Wassner SJ. Altered growth and protein turnover in rats fed sodium-deficient diets. *Pediatr Res* 1989;**26**:608–13.

67. Wassner SJ. The effect of sodium repletion on growth and protein turnover in sodium-depleted rats. *Pediatr Nephrol* 1991;**5**:501–4.

68. Heinly MM, Wassner SJ. The effect of isolated chloride depletion on growth and protein turnover in young rats. *Pediatr Nephrol* 1994;**8**:555–60.

69. Grossman H, Duggan E, McCamman S, Welchert E, Hellerstein S. The dietary chloride deficiency syndrome. *Pediatrics* 1980;**66**:366–74.

70. Mitch WE, May RC, Kelly RA, Maroni BJ, Hara Y, Druml WJ, *et al*. Protein metabolism in uremia. In: Davison AM, editor. *Nephrology*. Vol. II. London: Bailliere Tindall; 1988. p. 1003–10.

71. May RC, Hara Y, Kelly RA, Block KP, Buse MG, Mitch WE. Branched-chain amino acid metabolism in rat muscle: abnormal regulation in acidosis. *Am J Physiol* 1987;**252**:712–18.

72. May RC, Kelly RA, Mitch WE. Metabolic acidosis stimulates protein degradation in rat muscle by a glucocorticoid-dependent mechanism. *J Clin Invest* 1986;**77**:614–21.

73. Williams B, Layward E, Walls J. Skeletal muscle degradation and nitrogen wasting in rats with chronic metabolic acidosis. *Clin Sci* 1991;**80**:457–62.

74. Bailey JL, Wang X, England BK, Price SR, Ding X, Mitch WE. The acidosis of chronic renal failure activates muscle proteolysis in rats by augmenting transcription of genes encoding proteins of the ATP-dependent ubiquitin-proteasome pathway. *J Clin Invest* 1996;**97**:1447–53.

75. Challa A, Krieg RJ, Jr., Thabet MA, Veldhuis JD, Chan JC. Metabolic acidosis inhibits growth hormone secretion in rats: mechanism of growth retardation. *Am J Physiol* 1993;**265**:547–53.

76. Challa A, Chan W, Krieg RJ, Jr., Thabet MA, Liu F, Hintz RL, *et al*. Effect of metabolic acidosis on the expression of insulin-like growth factor and growth hormone receptor. *Kidney Int* 1993;**44**:1224–7.

77. Brüngger M, Hulter HN, Krapf R. Effect of chronic metabolic acidosis on the growth hormone/IGF-1 endocrine axis: new cause of growth hormone insensitivity in humans. *Kidney Int* 1997;**51**:216–21.

78. Kattamis CA, Kattamis AC. Management of thalassemias: growth and development, hormone substitution, vitamin supplementation, and vaccination. *Semin Hematol* 1995;**32**:269–79.

79. Seidel C, Schaefer F, Walther U, Schärer K. The application of knemometry in renal disease: preliminary observations. *Pediatr Nephrol* 1991;**5**:467–71.

80. Schaefer F, André JL, Krug C, Messinger D, Scigalla P. Growth and skeletal maturation in dialysed children treated with recombinant human erythropoietin (rhEPO) – a multicenter study. *Pediatr Nephrol* 1991;**5**:C61.

81. Mehls O, Ritz E. Skeletal growth in experimental uremia. *Kidney Int Suppl* 1983;**15**:S53–62.

82. Mehls O, Ritz E, Kreusser W, Krempien B. Renal osteodystrophy in uraemic children. *Clin Endocrinol Metab* 1980;**9**:151–76.

83. Mehls O, Ritz E, Gilli G, Wangdak T, Krempien B. Effect of vitamin D on growth in experimental uremia. *Am J Clin Nutr* 1978;**31**:1927–31.

84. Mehls O, Ritz E, Gilli G, Heinrich U. Role of hormonal disturbances in uremic growth failure. *Contrib Nephrol* 1986;**50**:119–29.

85. Chesney RW, Moorthy AV, Eisman JA, Jax DK, Mazess RB, DeLuca HF. Increased growth after long-term oral 1alpha, 25-vitamin D3 in childhood renal osteodystrophy. *N Engl J Med* 1978;**298**:238–42.

86. Chesney RW, Hamstra A, Jax DK, Mazess RB, DeLuca HF. Influence of long-term oral 1,25-vitamin D in childhood renal osteodystrophy. *Contrib Nephrol* 1980;**18**:55–71.

87. Kreusser W, Weinkauf R, Mehls O, Ritz E. Effect of parathyroid hormone, calcitonin and growth hormone on cAMP content of growth cartilage in experimental uremia. *Eur J Clin Invest* 1982; **12**:337–43.

88. Klaus G, von Eichel B, May T, Hügel U, Mayer H, Ritz E, *et al.* Synergistic effects of parathyroid hormone and 1,25-dihydroxyvitamin D3 on proliferation and vitamin D receptor expression of rat growth cartilage cells. *Endocrinology* 1994;**135**:1307–15.

89. Schmitt CP, Hessing S, Oh J, Weber L, Ochlich P, Mehls O. Intermittent administration of parathyroid hormone (1-37) improves growth and bone mineral density in uremic rats. *Kidney Int* 2000;**57**:1484–92.

90. Kuizon BD, Goodman WG, Jüppner H, Boechat I, Nelson P, Gales B, *et al.* Diminished linear growth during intermittent calcitriol therapy in children undergoing CCPD. *Kidney Int* 1998;**53**:205–11.

91. Krempien B, Mehls O, Ritz E. Morphological studies on pathogenesis of epiphyseal slipping in uremic children. *Virchows Arch (A)* 1974;**362**: 129–43.

92. Mehls O, Ritz E, Krempien B, Gilli G, Link K, Willich W, *et al.* Slipped epiphyses in renal osteodystrophy. *Arch Dis Child* 1975;**50**:545–54.

93. Mehls O, Ritz E, Oppermann HC, Guignard JP. Femoral head necrosis in uremic children without steroid treatment or transplantation. *J Pediatr* 1981;**6**:926–9.

94. Tejani A, Fine RN, Alexander S, Harmon W, Stablein D. Factors predictive of sustained growth in children after renal transplantation. The North American Pediatric Renal Transplant Cooperative Study. *J Pediatr* 1993;**122**:397–402.

95. Emmanouel DS, Lindheimer MD, Katz AI. Pathogenesis of endocrine abnormalities in uremia. *Endocr Rev* 1980;**1**:28–44.

96. Rabkin R, Unterhalter SA, Duckworth WC. Effect of prolonged uremia on insulin metabolism by isolated liver and muscle. *Kidney Int* 1979; **16**:433–9.

97. Hruska KA, Korkor A, Martin K, Slatopolsky E. Peripheral metabolism of intact parathyroid hormone. *J Clin Invest* 1981;**67**:885–92.

98. Powell DR, Lee PDK, Chang D, Liu F, Hintz RL. Antiserum developed for the E peptide region of insulin-like growth factor IA prohormone recognizes a serum protein by both immunoblot and radioimmunoassay. *J Clin Endocrinol Metab* 1987;**65**:868–75.

99. Zilker TR, Rebel C, Kopp KF, Wahl K, Ermler R, Heinzel G, *et al.* Kinetics of biosynthetic human proinsulin in patients with terminal renal insufficiency. *Horm Metab Res Suppl* 1988; **18**:43–8.

100. Lim VS, Fang VS, Katz AI, Refetoff S. Thyroid dysfunction in chronic renal failure. *J Clin Invest* 1977;**60**:522–34.

101. Kishore BK, Arakawa M, Geiyo F. Altered glycosylation and sialylation of serum proteins and lipid bound sialic acids in chronic renal failure. *Postgrad Med J* 1983;**59**:551–5.

102. Schaefer F, Seidel C, Mitchell R, Schärer K, Robertson WR, Cooperative Study on Pubertal Development In Chronic Renal Failure. Pulsatile immunoreactive and bioactive luteinizing hormone secretion in pubertal patients with chronic renal failure. *Pediatr Nephrol* 1991; **5**:566–71.

103. Postel-Vinay MC, Tar A, Crosnier H, Broyer M, Rappaport R, Tönshoff B, *et al.* Plasma growth-hormone binding is low in uremic children. *Pediatr Nephrol* 1991;**5**:545–7.

104. Lee PD, Hintz RL, Sperry JB, Baxter RC, Powell DR. IGF binding proteins in growth-retarded children with chronic renal failure. *Pediatr Res* 1989;**26**:308–15.

105. Blum WF, Ranke MB, Kietzmann K, Tönshoff B, Mehls O. Excess of IGF-binding proteins in chronic renal failure: evidence for relative GH resistance and inhibition of somatomedin activity. In: Drop SLS; Hintz RL, editors. *Insulin-like growth factor binding proteins.* Amsterdam: Elsevier Science Publishers BV; 1989. p. 93–9.

106. Smith D, Defronzo RA. Insulin resistance in uremia mediated by postbinding defects. *Kidney Int* 1982;**22**:54–62.

107. Handelsman DJ. Hypothalamic-pituitary gonadal dysfunction in renal failure, dialysis and renal transplantation. *Endocr Rev* 1985;**6**:151–82.

108. Corvol B, Bertagna X, Bedrossian J. Increased steroid metabolic clearance rate in anephric patients. *Acta Endocrinol (Copenh)* 1974;**75**:756–62.

109. Stewart-Bentley M, Gans D, Horton R. Regulation of gonadal function in uremia. *Metabolism* 1974;**23**:1065–72.

110. Oertel PJ, Lichtwald K, Häfner S, Rauh W, Schönberg D, Schärer K. Hypothalamo-pituitary-gonadal axis in children with chronic renal failure. *Kidney Int* 1983;**24**:34–9.

111. Ferraris J, Saenger P, Levine L, New M, Pang S, Saxena BB, *et al.* Delayed puberty in males with chronic renal failure. *Kidney Int* 1980;**18**:344–50.

112. Schärer KSP, Cooperative Study On Pubertal Development In Chronic Renal Failure. Adrenal androgens in plasma of boys with chronic renal failure. *Pediatr Nephrol* 1992;**6**:C179.

113. Schärer K, Broyer M, Vecsei P, Roger M, Arnold-Schwender E, Usberti J. Damage to testicular function in chronic renal failure of children. *Proc Eur Dial Transplant Assoc* 1980;**17**:725–9.

114. Roger M, Broyer M, Schärer K, Castanier M, Usberti J. Gonadotropins et androgènes plasmatiques chez les garcons traités pour insuffisance rénale chronique. *Path Biol* 1981;**29**:378–9.

115. Garnier P, Naret C, Blacker C, Delons S. [Results of hormonal studies in 23 adolescents with renal failure treated by chronic dialysis]. *Pathol Biol Paris* 1988;**36**:988–94.

116. Belgorosky A, Ferraris JR, Ramirez JA, Jasper H, Rivarola MA. Serum sex hormone-binding globulin and serum nonsex hormone-binding globulin-bound testosterone fractions in pre-pubertal boys with chronic renal failure. *J Clin Endocrinol Metab* 1991;**73**:107–10.

117. Schaefer FH. Cooperative study on pubertal development in chronic renal failure. Pulsatile growth hormone secretion in peripubertal patients with chronic renal failure. *J Pediatr* 1991;**119**:568–77.

118. Gupta D, Bundschu HD. Testosterone and its binding in the plasma of male subjects with chronic renal failure. *Clin Chim Acta* 1972;**36**:479–86.

119. van Kammen E, Thijssen JH, Schwarz F. Sex hormones in male patients with chronic renal failure. I. The production of testosterone and androstenedione. *Clin Endocrinol* 1978;**8**:7–14.

120. Kreusser W, Spiegelberg U, Sis J, Wagner D, Ritz E. Hypergonadotroper Hypogonadismus bei Niereninsuffizienz - eine Folge gestörter cAMP-Bildung. *Verh Dtsch Ges Inn Med* 1978;**84**:1446–8.

121. Dunkel L, Raivio T, Laine J, Holmberg C. Circulating luteinizing hormone receptor inhibitor(s) in boys with chronic renal failure. *Kidney Int* 1997;**51**:777–84.

122. Mitchell R, Schaefer F, Morris ID, Schärer K, Sun JG, Robertson WR. Elevated serum immunoreactive inhibin levels in pubertal boys with chronic renal failure. *Clin Endocrinol* 1993;**39**:27–33.

123. Lim VS, Sievertsen G, Kathpalie S, Frohman LA. Ovarian function in women with chronic renal failure: evidence suggesting central and end organ disturbances. *Kidney Int* 1978;**14**:679.

124. Lim VS, Henriquez C, Sievertsen G, Frohman LA. Ovarian function in chronic renal failure: evidence suggesting hypothalamic anovulation. *Ann Inter Med* 1980;**93**:21–7.

125. Ferraris JR, Domene HM, Escobar ME, Caletti MG, Ramirez JA, Rivarola MA. Hormonal profile in pubertal females with chronic renal failure: before and under haemodialysis and after renal transplantation. *Acta Endocrinol (Copenh)* 1987;**115**:289–96.

126. Schärer K, Schaefer F, Trott M, Kassmann K, Gilli G, Gerhard I, et al. Pubertal development in children with chronic renal failure. In: Schärer K, editor. *Growth and endocrine changes in children and adolescents with chronic renal failure.* Pediatric and Adolescent Endocrinology. Vol. 22. Basel: Karger; 1989. p. 151–68.

127. Swamy AP, Woolf PD, Cestero RVM. Hypothalamic-pituitary-ovarian axis in uremic women. *J Lab Clin Med* 1979;**93**:1066–72.

128. Marder HK, Srivastava LS, Burstein S. Hypergonadotropism in peripubertal boys with chronic renal failure. *Pediatrics* 1983;**72**:384–9.

129. Blackman M, Weintraub B, Kourides I, Solano J, Santner T, Rosen S. Discordant elevation of the common alpha-subunit of the glycoprotein hormones compared to beta-subunits in serum of uremic patients. *J Clin Endocrinol Metab* 1981;**53**:39–48.

130. Holdsworth S, Atkins RC, de Kretser DM. The pituitary-testicular axis in men with chronic renal failure. *N Engl J Med* 1977;**296**:1245–9.

131. Corley KP, Valk TW, Kelch RP, Marshall JC. Estimation of GnRH pulse amplitude during pubertal development. *Pediatr Res* 1981;**15**:157–62.

132. Veldhuis JD, Carlson ML, Johnson ML. The pituitary gland secretes in bursts: appraising the nature of glandular secretory impulses by simultaneous multiple-parameter deconvolution of plasma hormone concentrations. *Proc Natl Acad Sci U S A* 1987;**84**:7686–90.

133. Schaefer F, Veldhuis JD, Robertson WR, Dunger D, Schärer K. Immunoreactive and bioactive luteinizing hormone in pubertal patients with chronic renal failure. Cooperative Study Group on Pubertal Development in Chronic Renal Failure. *Kidney Int* 1994;**45**:1465–76.

134. Schaefer F, Daschner M, Veldhuis JD, Oh J, Qadri F, Schärer K. *In vivo* alterations in the gonadotropin-releasing hormone pulse generator and the secretion and clearance of luteinizing hormone in the uremic castrate rat. *Neuroendocrinology* 1994;**59**:285–96.

135. Dong Q, Handelsman DJ. Regulation of pulsatile luteinizing hormone secretion in experimental uremia. *Endocrinology* 1991;**128**:1218–22.

136. Talbot JA, Rodger RSC, Robertson WR. Pulsatile bioactive luteinising hormone secretion in men with chronic renal failure and following renal transplantation. *Nephron* 1990;**56**:66–72.

137. Wibullaksanakul S, Handelsman DJ. Regulation of hypothalamic gonadotropin-releasing hormone secretion in experimental uremia: *in vitro* studies. *Neuroendocrinology* 1991;**54**:353–8.

138. Daschner M, Philippin B, Nguyen T, Wiesner RJ, Walz C, Sandow J, *et al.* Circulating inhibitor of gonadotropin releasing hormone secretion from hypothalamic neurons in uremia. *Kidney Int* 2002;**62**(5):1582–90.

139. Schaefer F, Vogel M, Kerkhoff G, Woitzik J, Daschner M, Mehls O. Experimental uremia affects hypothalamic amino acid neurotransmitter milieu. *J Am Soc Nephrol* 2001;**12**:1218–27.

140. Robertson WR, Lambert A, Loveridge N. The role of modern bioassays in clinical endocrinology. *Clin Endocrinol (Oxf)* 1987;**27**:259–78.

141. Celani MF, Montanini V, Baraghini GF, Carani C, Cioni K, Resentini M, et al. Biological and immunological profiles of serum luteinizing hormone (LH) during male sexual maturation. *Acta Med Auxol* 1983;**15**:195–204.

142. Schaefer F, Mitchell R, Schärer K, Robertson WR. Gonadotrophin secretion in pubertal children on dialysis or after renal transplantation. *J Endocrinol (Suppl)* 1989;**121**:230.

143. Giusti M, Perfumo F, Verrina E, Cavallero D, Piaggio G, Gusmano R, et al. Biological activity of luteinizing hormone in uremic children: spontaneous nocturnal secretion and changes after administration of exogenous pulsatile luteinizing hormone releasing hormone. *Pediatr Nephrol* 1991;**5**:559–65.

144. Mitchell R, Bauerfeld C, Schaefer F, Schärer K, Robertson WR. Less acidic forms of luteinizing hormone are associated with lower testosterone secretion in men on hemodialysis treatment. *Clin Endocrinol* 1994;**41**:65–73.

145. Gomez F, de la Cueva R, Wauters J, Lemarchand-Beraud T. Endocrine abnormalities in patients undergoing long-term hemodialysis – the role of prolactin. *Am J Med* 1980;**68**:522–30.

146. Sievertsen GD, Lim VS, Natawatase C, Frohman LA. Metabolic clearance and secretion rates of human prolactin in normal subjects and in patients with chronic renal failure. *J Clin Endocrinol Metab* 1980;**50**:846–52.

147. Winters SJ, Troen P. Altered pulsatile secretion of luteinising hormone in hypogonadal men with hyperprolactinemia. *Clin Endocrinol* 1984;**21**:257–63.

148. Schmitz O. Absence of diurnal plasma prolactin rhythm in diabetic and non-diabetic uremic patients. *Acta Endocrinol (Copenh)* 1984;**105**:173–8.

149. Biasioli S, Mazzali A, Foroni R, D'Andrea G, Feriani M, Chiaramonte S, et al. Chronobiological variations of prolactin (PRL) in chronic renal failure (CRF). *Clin Nephrol* 1988;**30**:86–92.

150. Czernichow P, Dauzet MC, Broyer M, Rappaport R. Abnormal TSH, PRL and GH response to TSH releasing factor in chronic renal failure. *J Clin Endocrinol Metab* 1976;**43**:630–7.

151. Ramirez GO. Abnormalities in the regulation of prolactin in patients with chronic renal failure. J *Clin Endocrinol Metab* 1977;**45**:658–61.

152. Bommer J, Ritz E, del Pozo E, Bommer G. Improved sexual function in male haemodialysis patients on bromocriptine. *Lancet* 1979;**2**:496–7.

153. Ruilope L, Garcia-Robles R, Paya C, de-Villa LF, Miranda B, Morales JM, et al. Influence of lisuride, a dopaminergic agonist, on the sexual function of male patients with chronic renal failure. *Am J Kidney Dis* 1985;**5**:182–5.

154. Verbeelen D, Vanhaelst L, van Steirteghem AC, Sennesael J. Effect of 1,25-dihydroxyvitamin D3 on plasma prolactin in patients with renal failure on regular dialysis treatment. *J Endocrinol Invest* 1983;**6**:359–62.

155. Schaefer RM, Kokot F, Kuerner B, Zech M, Heidland A. Normalization of serum prolactin levels in hemodialysis patients on recombinant human erythropoietin. *Int J Artif Organs* 1989;**12**:445–9.

156. Le Roith D, Bondy C, Yakar S, Liu JL, Butler A. The somatomedin hypothesis: 2001. *Endocr Rev* 2001;**22**:53–74.

157. Green H, Morikawa M, Nixon T. A dual effector theory of growth-hormone action. *Differentiation* 1985;**29**:195–8.

158. Isaksson OG, Lindahl A, Nilsson A, Isgaard J. Mechanism of the stimulatory effect of growth hormone on longitudinal bone growth. *Endocr Rev* 1987;**8**:426–38.

159. Clemmons DR, Klibanski A, Underwood LE. Reduction of serum immunoreactive somatomedin C during fasting in humans. *J Clin Endocrinol Metab* 1981;**53**:1247–50.

160. Isley WL, Underwood LE, Clemmons DR. Dietary components that regulate serum somatomedin-C concentrations in humans. *J Clin Invest* 1983; **71**:175–82.

161. Strauss DS, Takemoto CD. Effect of fasting on insulin-like growth factor-I (IGF-I) and growth hormone receptor mRNA levels and IGF-I gene transcription in rat liver. *Mol Endocrinol* 1990;**4**:91–100.

162. Thissen JP, Triest S, Moats-Staats BM. Evidence that pretranslational and translational defects decrease serum insulin-like growth factor-I concentrations during dietary protein restriction. *Endocrinology* 1991;**129**:429–35.

163. Parker MW, Johnson AJ, Rogol AD, Kaiser DL, Blizzard RM. Effect of testosterone on somatomedin-C concentrations in prepubertal boys. *J Clin Endocrinol Metab* 1984;**58**:87–90.

164. Yakar S, Liu JL, Stannard B, Butler A, Accili D, Sauer B, et al. Normal growth and development in the absence of hepatic insulin-like growth factor I. *Proc Natl Acad Sci U S A* 1999;**96**:7324–9.

165. Sjogren K, Liu JL, Blad K, Skrtic S, Vidal O, Wallenius V, et al. Liver-derived insulin-like growth factor I (IGF-I) is the principal source of IGF-I in blood but is not required for postnatal body growth in mice. *Proc Natl Acad Sci U S A* 1999;**96**:7088–92.

166. Ueki I, Ooi GT, Tremblay ML, Hurst KR, Bach LA, Boisclair YR. Inactivation of the acid labile

subunit gene in mice results in mild retardation of postnatal growth despite profound disruptions in the circulating insulin-like growth factor system. *Proc Natl Acad Sci U S A* 2000;**97**:6868–73.

167. Hoffenberg R, Howell A, Epstein S, Pimstone BL, Fryklund L, Hall K, *et al.* Increasing growth with raised circulating somatomedin but normal immunoassayable growth hormone. *Clin Endocrinol (Oxf)* 1977;**6**:443–8.

168. Shalet SM, Price DA, Beardwell CG, Jones PH, Pearson D. Normal growth despite abnormalities of growth hormone secretion in children treated for acute leukemia. *J Pediatr* 1979;**94**:719–22.

169. Samaan NA, Freeman RM. Growth hormone levels in severe renal failure. *Metabolism* 1970;**19**:102–13.

170. Pimstone BL, Le Roith D, Epstein S, Kronheim S. Disappearance rates of serum growth hormone after intravenous somatostatin in renal and liver disease. *J Clin Endocrinol Metab* 1975;**41**:392–3.

171. Davidson M, Fisher M, Dabir-Vaziri N, Schaffer M. Effect of protein intake and dialysis on the abnormal growth hormone, glucose, and insulin homeostasis in uremia. *Metabolism* 1976;**25**:455–64.

172. Johnson V, Maack T. Renal extraction, filtration absorption, and catabolism of growth hormone. *Am J Physiol* 1977;**233**:F185–96.

173. Tönshoff B, Veldhuis JD, Heinrich U, Mehls O. Deconvolution analysis of spontaneous nocturnal growth hormone secretion in prepubertal children with chronic renal failure. *Pediatr Res* 1995;**37**:86–93.

174. Veldhuis JD, Iranmanesh A, Wilkowski MJ, Samojlik E. Neuroendocrine alterations in the somatotropic and lactotropic axes in uremic men. *Eur J Endocrinol* 1994;**131**:489–98.

175. Schaefer F, Veldhuis JD, Jones J, Schärer K. Alterations in growth hormone secretion and clearance in peripubertal boys with chronic renal failure and after renal transplantation. *J Clin Endocrinol Metab* 1994;**78**:1298–306.

176. Haffner D, Schaefer F, Girard J, Ritz E, Mehls O. Metabolic clearance of recombinant human growth hormone in health and chronic renal failure. *J Clin Invest* 1994;**93**:1163–71.

177. Leung DW, Spencer SA, Cachianes G, Hammnonds RG, Collins C, Hentzel WJ, *et al.* Growth hormone receptor and serum binding protein: Purification, cloning and expression. *Nature* 1987;**330**:537–43.

178. Tönshoff B, Cronin MJ, Reichert M, Haffner D, Wingen AM, Blum WF, *et al.* Reduced concentration of serum growth hormone (GH)-binding protein in children with chronic renal failure: correlation with GH insensitivity. *J Clin Endocrinol Metab* 1997;**82**:1007–13.

179. Baumann G, Shaw MA, Amburn K. Regulation of plasma growth hormone-binding proteins in health and disease. *Metabolism* 1989;**38**:683–89.

180. Maheshwari HG, Rifkin I, Butler J, Norman M. Growth hormone binding protein in patients with renal failure. *Acta Endocrinol.* 1992;**127**:485–8.

181. Kagan A, Zadik Z, Gertler A, Ulman M, Bar-Khayim Y. Serum concentrations and peritoneal loss of growth hormone and growth-hormone-binding protein activity in older adults undergoing continuous ambulatory peritoneal dialysis: comparison with haemodialysis and normal subjects. *Nephrol Dial Transplant* 1993;**8**:352–6.

182. Carlsson LMS, Attie KM, Compton PG, Vitangcol RV, Merimee TJ, The National Cooperative Growth Study. Reduced concentration of serum growth hormone-binding protein in children with idiopathic short stature. *J Clin Endocrinol Metab* 1994;**78**:1325–30.

183. Ho KYY, Jorgensen JOL, Valiontis E. Different modes of growth hormone (GH) administration do not change GH binding protein activity in man. *Clin Endocrinol* 1993;**38**:143–7.

184. Davila N, Alcaniz J, Salto L, Estrada J, Barcelo B, Baumann G. Serum growth hormone-binding protein is unchanged in adult panhypo-pituitarism. *J Clin Endocrinol Metab* 1994;**79**:1347–50.

185. Martha PM, Jr., Reiter EO, Davila N, Shaw MA, Holcombe JJ, Baumann G. Serum growth hormone-binding protein/receptor: an important determinant of growth hormone responsiveness. *J Clin Endocrinol Metab* 1992;**75**:1464–9.

186. Tauber M, Portal HB, Sallerin-Caute B, Rochiccioli P, Bastide R. Differential regulation of serum growth hormone (GH)-binding protein during continuous infusion versus daily injection of recombinant human GH in GH-deficient children. *J Clin Endocrinol Metab* 1993;**76**:1135–9.

187. Chan W, Valerie KC, Chan JCM. Expression of insulin-like growth factor-1 in uremic rats: Growth hormone resistance and nutritional intake. *Kidney Int* 1993;**43**:790–5.

188. Tönshoff B, Eden S, Weiser E, Carlsson B, Robinson IC, Blum WF, *et al.*Mehls O. Reduced hepatic growth hormone (GH) receptor gene expression and increased plasma GH binding protein in experimental uremia. *Kidney Int* 1994;**45**:1085–92.

189. Schaefer F, Chen Y, Tsao T, Nouri P, Rabkin R. Impaired JAK-STAT signal transduction contributes to growth hormone resistance in chronic uremia. *J Clin Invest* 2001;**108**:467–75.

190. Carter-Su C, Rui L, Herington J. Role of the tyrosine kinase JAK2 in signal transduction by growth hormone. *Pediatr Nephrol* 2000;**14**:550–7.

191. Udy GB, Towers RP, Snell RG, Wilkins RJ, Park SH, Ram PR, *et al.* Requirement of STAT5b for sexual dimorphism of body growth rates and liver gene expression. *Proc Natl Acad Sci U S A* 1997;**94**:7239–44.

192. Teglund S, McKay C, Schuetz E, van Deursen JM, Stravopodis D, Wang D, et al. STAT5a and STAT5b proteins have essential and nonessential, or redundant, roles in cytokine responses. *Cell* 1998;**93**:841–50.

193. Touw IP, De Koning JP, Ward AC, Hermans MH. Signaling mechanisms of cytokine receptors and their perturbances in disease. *Mol Cell Endocrinol* 2000;**160**:1–9.

194. Greenhalgh CJ, Hilton DJ. Negative regulation of cytokine signaling. *J Leukoc Biol* 2001;**70**:348–56

195. Davey HW, McLachlan MJ, Wilkins RJ, Hilton DJ, Adams TE. STAT5b mediates the GH-induced expression of SOCS-2 and SOCS-3 mRNA in the liver. *Mol Cell Endocrinol* 1999;**158**:111–6.

196. Ram PR, Waxman DJ. SOCS/CIS protein inhibition of growth hormone-stimulated STAT5 signaling by multiple mechanisms. *J Biol Chem* 1999;**275**:35553–61.

197. Tollet-Egnell P, Flores-Morales A, Stavreus-Evers A, Sahlin L, Norstedt G. Growth hormone regulation of SOCS-2, SOCS-3, and CIS messenger ribonucleic acid expression in the rat. *Endocrinology* 1999;**140**:3693–704.

198. Metcalf D, Greenhalgh CJ, Viney E, Wilson TA, Starr R, Nicola NA, et al. Gigantism in mice lacking suppressor of cytokine signalling-2. *Nature* 2000;**405**:1069–73.

199. Paul C, Seiliez I, Thissen JP, Le Cam A. Regulation of expression of the rat SOCS-3 gene in hepatocytes by growth hormone, interleukin-6 and glucocorticoids mRNA analysis and promoter characterization. *Eur J Biochem* 2000;**267**:5849–57.

200. Mao Y, Ling PR, Fitzgibbons TP, McCowen KC, Frick GP, Bistrian BR, et al. Endotoxin-induced inhibition of growth hormone receptor signaling in rat liver *in vivo. Endocrinology* 1999;**140**:5505–15.

201. Bergad PL, Schwarzenberg SJ, Humbert JT, Morrison M, Amarasinghe S, Towle HC, et al. Inhibition of growth hormone action in models of inflammation. *Am J Physiol Cell Physiol* 2000;**279**:C1906–17.

202. Kaysen GA. The microinflammatory state in uremia: causes and potential consequences. *J Am Soc Nephrol* 2001;**12**:1549–57.

203. Tönshoff B, Blum WF, Wingen AM, Mehls O. Serum insulin-like growth factors (IGFs) and IGF binding proteins 1, 2, and 3 in children with chronic renal failure: relationship to height and glomerular filtration rate. *J Clin Endocrinol Metab* 1995;**80**:2684–91.

204. Tönshoff B, Blum WF, Mehls O. Serum insulin-like growth factors and their binding proteins in children with end-stage renal disease. *Pediatr Nephrol* 1996;**10**:269–74.

205. Ulinski T, Mohan S, Kiepe D, Blum WF, Wingen AM, Mehls O et al. Serum insulin-like growth factor binding protein (IGFBP)-4 and IGFBP-5 in children with chronic renal failure: relationship to growth and glomerular filtration rate. *Pediatr Nephrol* 2000;**14**:589–97.

206. Phillips LS, Fusco AC, Unterman TG, Del Greco F. Somatomedin inhibitor in uremia. *J Clin Endocrinol Metab* 1984;**59**:764–72.

207. Blum WF, Ranke MB, Kietzmann K, Tönshoff B, Mehls O. Growth hormone resistance and inhibition of somatomedin activity by excess of insulin-like growth factor binding protein in uraemia. *Pediatr Nephrol* 1991;**5**:539–44.

208. Frystyk J, Ivarsen P, Skjaerbaek C, Flyvbjerg A, Pedersen EB, Orskov H. Serum-free insulin-like growth factor I correlates with clearance in patients with chronic renal failure. *Kidney Int* 1999;**56**:2076–84.

209. Baxter RC. Insulin-like growth factor (IGF)-binding proteins: interactions with IGFs and intrinsic bioactivities. *Am J Physiol Endocrinol Metab* 2000;**278**:E967–76.

210. Hwa V, Oh Y, Rosenfeld RG. The insulin-like growth factor-binding protein (IGFBP) super-family. *Endocr Rev* 1999;**20**:761–87.

211. Lee PD, Giudice LC, Conover CA, Powell DR. Insulin-like growth factor binding protein-1: recent findings and new directions. *Proc Soc Exp Biol Med* 1997;**216**:319–57.

212. Powell DR, Rosenfeld RG, Sperry JB, Baker BK, Hintz RL. Serum concentrations of insulin-like growth factor (IGF)-1, IGF-2 and unsaturated somatomedin carrier proteins in children with chronic renal failure. *Am J Kidney Dis* 1987;**10**:287–92.

213. Liu F, Powell DR, Hintz RL. Characterization of insulin-like growth factor binding proteins in human serum from patients with chronic renal failure. *J Clin Endocrinol Metab* 1990;**70**:620–28.

214. Baxter RC, Martin JL, Beniac VA. High molecular weight insulin-like growth factor binding protein complex. *J Biol Chem* 1989;**264**:11843–8

215. Powell DR, Liu F, Baker BK, Hintz RL, Durham SK, Brewer ED, et al. Insulin-like growth factor binding protein-6 levels are elevated in serum of children with chronic renal failure: a report of the Southwest Pediatric Nephrology Study Group. *J Clin Endocrinol Metab* 1997;**82**:2978–84.

216. Powell DR, Liu F, Baker BK, Lee PD, Belsha CW, Brewer ED, Hintz RL. Characterization of insulin-like growth factor binding protein-3 in chronic renal failure serum. *Pediatr Res* 1993;**33**:136–43.

217. Powell DR, Liu F, Baker BK, Hintz RL, Lee PD, Durham SK, et al. Modulation of growth factors by growth hormone in children with chronic renal failure. The Southwest Pediatric Nephrology Study Group. *Kidney Int* 1997;**51**:1970–79.

218. Powell DR, Durham SK, Brewer ED, Frane JW, Watkins SL, Hogg RJ, Mohan S. Effects of chronic

renal failure and growth hormone on serum levels of insulin-like growth factor-binding protein-4 (IGFBP-4) and IGFBP-5 in children: a report of the Southwest Pediatric Nephrology Study Group. *J Clin Endocrinol Metab* 1999;**84**:596–601.

219. Durham SK, Mohan S, Liu F, Baker BK, Lee PD, Hintz RL, *et al.* Bioactivity of a 29-kilodalton insulin-like growth factor binding protein-3 fragment present in excess in chronic renal failure serum. *Pediatr Res* 1997;**42**:335–41.

220. Wühl E, Haffner D, Nissel R, Schaefer F, Mehls O. Short dialyzed children respond less to growth hormone than patients prior to dialysis. German Study Group for Growth Hormone Treatment in Chronic Renal Failure. *Pediatr Nephrol* 1996;**10**: 294–8.

221. Blum WF. Insulin-like growth factors (IGFs) and IGF binding proteins in chronic renal failure: Evidence for reduced secretion of IGFs. *Acta Paediatr Scand Suppl* 1991;**379**:24–31.

222. Tönshoff B, Powell DR, Zhao D, Durham SK, Coleman ME, Domene HM, *et al.* Decreased hepatic insulin-like growth factor (IGF)-I and increased IGF binding protein-1 and -2 gene expression in experimental uremia. *Endocrinology* 1997;**138**:938–46.

223. Holly JM, Claffey DC, Cwyfan-Hughes SC, Frost VJ, Yateman ME. Proteases acting on IGFBPs: their occurrence and physiological significance. *Growth Regul* 1993;**3**:88–91.

224. Lee DY, Park SK, Yorgin PD, Cohen P, Oh Y, Rosenfeld RG. Alteration in insulin-like growth factor-binding proteins (IGFBPs) and IGFBP-3 protease activity in serum and urine from acute and chronic renal failure. *J Clin Endocrinol Metab* 1994;**79**:1376–82.

225. Ooi GT, Tseng LYH, Rechler MM. Post-transcriptional regulation of insulin-like growth factor binding protein-2 mRNA in diabetic liver. *Biochem Biophys Res Commun* 1992;**189**: 1031–7.

226. Margot JB, Binkert C, Mary JL, Landwehr J, Heinrich G, Schwander J. A low molecular weight insulin-like growth factor binding protein from rat: cDNA cloning and tissue distribution of its messenger RNA. *Mol Endocrinol* 1989;**3**: 1053–60.

227. Binoux M, Hossenlopp P. Insulin-like growth factor (IGF) and IGF-binding proteins: comparison of human serum and lymph. *J Clin Endocrinol Metab* 1988;**67**:509–14.

228. Kale AS, Liu F, Hintz RL, Baker BK, Brewer ED, Lee PD, *et al.* Characterization of insulin-like growth factors and their binding proteins in peritoneal dialysate. *Pediatr Nephrol* 1996;**10**: 467–73.

229. Burch WM, Correa J, Shively JE, Powell DR. The 25-kilodalton insulin-like growth factor (IGF)-binding protein inhibits both basal and IGF-I-mediated growth of chick embryo pelvic cartilage

in vitro. J Clin Endocrinol Metab 1990;**70**: 173–80.

230. Standker L, Braulke T, Mark S, Mostafavi H, Meyer M, Honing S, *et al.* Partial IGF affinity of circulating N- and C-terminal fragments of human insulin-like growth factor binding protein-4 (IGFBP-4) and the disulfide bonding pattern of the C-terminal IGFBP-4 domain. *Biochemistry* 2000;**39**:5082–8.

231. Standker L, Wobst P, Mark S, Forssmann WG. Isolation and characterization of circulating 13-kDa C-terminal fragments of human insulin-like growth factor binding protein-5. FEBS *Lett* 1998; **441**:281–6.

232. Kiepe D, Ulinski T, Powell DR, Durham SK, Mehls O, Tönshoff B. Differential effects of IGFBP-1, -2, -3, and -6 on cultured growth plate chondrocytes. *Kidney Int* 2002;**62**(5):1591–6000.

233. Kiepe D, Andress DL, Mohan S, Standker L, Ulinski T, Himmele R, *et al.* Intact IGF-binding protein-4 and -5 and their respective fragments isolated from chronic renal failure serum differentially modulate IGF-I actions in cultured growth plate chondrocytes. *J Am Soc Nephrol* 2001;**12**:2400–10.

234. Rajkumar K, Barron D, Lewitt MS, Murphy LJ. Growth retardation and hyperglycemia in insulin-like growth factor binding protein-1 transgenic mice. *Endocrinology* 1995;**136**:4029–34.

235. Gay E, Seurin D, Babajko S, Doublier S, Cazillis M, Binoux M. Liver-specific expression of human insulin-like growth factor binding protein-1 in transgenic mice: repercussions on reproduction, ante- and perinatal mortality and postnatal growth. *Endocrinology* 1997;**138**: 2937–47.

236. Hoeflich A, Wu M, Mohan S, Foll J, Wanke R, Froehlich T, *et al.* Overexpression of insulin-like growth factor-binding protein-2 in transgenic mice reduces postnatal body weight gain. *Endocrinology* 1999;**140**:5488–96.

237. Modric T, Silha JV, Shi Z, Gui Y, Suwanichkul A, Durham SK, *et al.* Phenotypic manifestations of insulin-like growth factor-binding protein-3 overexpression in transgenic mice. *Endocrinology* 2001;**142**:1958–67.

238. Cox GN, McDermott MJ, Merkel E, Stroh CA, Ko SC, Squires CH, *et al.* Recombinant human insulin-like growth factor (IGF)-binding protein-1 inhibits somatic growth stimulated by IGF-I and growth hormone in hypophysectomized rats. *Endocrinology* 1994;**135**:1913–20.

239. Hoeflich A, Nedbal S, Blum WF, Erhad M, Lahm H, Bren G, *et al.* Growth inhibition in giant growth hormone transgenic mice by overexpression of insulin-like growth factor-binding protein-2. *Endocrinology* 2001;**142**:1889–98.

240. Tönshoff B, Mehls O, Heinrich U, Blum WF, Ranke MB, Schauer A. Growth-stimulating effects of recombinant human growth hormone

in children with end-stage renal disease. *J Pediatr* 1990;**4**:561–6.

241. Hokken-Koelega AC, Stijnen T, de Muinck Keizer-Schrama SM, Wit JM, Wolff ED, de Jong MC, *et al.* Placebo-controlled, double-blind, cross-over trial of growth hormone treatment in prepubertal children with chronic renal failure. *Lancet* 1991;**338**:585–90.

242. Powell DR, Durham SK, Liu F, Baker BK, Lee PD, Watkins SL, *et al.* The insulin-like growth factor axis and growth in children with chronic renal failure: a report of the Southwest Pediatric Nephrology Study Group. *J Clin Endocrinol Metab* 1998;**83**:1654–61

243. Hazel SJ, Gillespie CM, Moore RJ, Clark RG, Jureidini KF, Martin AA. Enhanced body growth in uremic rats treated with IGF-I and growth hormone in combination. *Kidney Int* 1994;**46**: 58–68.

244. Kovacs GT, Oh J, Kovacs J, Tönshoff B, Hunziker EB, Zapf J, *et al.* Growth promoting effects of growth hormone and IGF-I are additive in experimental uremia. *Kidney Int* 1996;**49**: 1413–21.

245. Guler HP, Schmid C, Zapf J, Froesch ER. Effects of recombinant insulin-like growth factor I on insulin secretion and renal function in normal human subjects. *Proc Natl Acad Sci U S A* 1989; **86**:2868–72.

246. Vijayan A, Franklin SC, Behrend T, Hammerman MR, Miller SB. Insulin-like growth factor I improves renal function in patients with end-stage chronic renal failure. *Am J Physiol* 1999;**276**: R929–34.

247. Loddick SA, Liu XJ, Lu ZX, Liu C, Behan DP, Chalmers DC, *et al.* Displacement of insulin-like growth factors from their binding proteins as a potential treatment for stroke. *Proc Natl Acad Sci U S A* 1998;**95**:1894–8.

248. Lowman HB, Chen YM, Skelton NJ, Mortensen DL, Tomlinson EE, Sadick MD, et al. Molecular mimics of insulin-like growth factor 1 (IGF-1) for inhibiting IGF-1: IGF-binding protein interactions. *Biochemistry* 1998;**37**:8870–8.

249. Roelfsema V, Lane MH, Clark RG. Insulin-like growth factor binding protein (IGFBP) displacers: relevance to the treatment of renal disease. *Pediatr Nephrol* 2000;**14**:584–8.

250. Tönshoff B, Mehls O. Interaction between glucocorticoids and the somatotrophic axis. *Acta Paediatr Suppl* 1996;**417**:72–5.

251. Veldhuis JD, Lizarralde G, Iranmanesh A. Divergent effects of short term glucocorticoid excess on the gonadotropic and somatotropic axes in normal men. *J Clin Endocrinol Metab* 1992;**74**:96–102.

252. Wehrenberg WB, Janowski BA, Piering AW, Culler F, Jones KL. Glucocorticoids: potent inhibitors and stimulators of growth hormone secretion. *Endocrinology* 1990;**126**:3200–3.

253. Gabrielsson BG, Carmignac DF, Flavell DM, Robinson ICAF. Steroid regulation of growth hormone (GH) receptor and GH-binding protein messenger ribonucleic acids in the rat. *Endocrinology* 1995;**136**:209–17.

254. Tönshoff B, Mehls O. Use of rhGH post transplant in children. In: Tejani A, Fine RN, editors. *Pediatric renal transplantation.* Tejani A, Fine RN (eds.) New York: John Wiley & Sons, Inc; 1994. p. 441–59.

255. Gourmelen M, Girard F, Binoux M. Serum somatomedin/insulin-like growth factor (IGF) and IGF carrier levels in patients with Cushing's syndrome or receiving glucocorticoid therapy. *J Clin Endocrinol Metab* 1982;**54**:885–92.

256. Tönshoff B, Haffner D, Mehls O, Dietz M, Ruder H, Blum WF et al. Efficacy and safety of growth hormone treatment in short children with renal allografts: three year experience. *Kidney Int* 1993; **44**:199–207.

257. Bang P, Degerblad M, Thoren M, Schwander J, Blum W, Hall K. Insulin-like growth factor (IGF) I and II and IGF binding protein (IGFBP) 1, 2 and 3 in serum from patients with Cushing's syndrome. *Acta Endocrinol* 1993;**128**:397–404.

258. Tönshoff B, Jux C, Mehls O. Glucocorticoids and growth. *Bailliere's Clin Paediatr Int Practice Res* 1996;**4**:309–32.

259. Jux C, Leiber K, Hugel U, Blum W, Ohlsson C, Klaus G, *et al.* Dexamethasone impairs growth hormone (GH)-stimulated growth by suppression of local insulin-like growth factor (IGF)-I production and expression of GH- and IGF-I-receptor in cultured rat chondrocytes. *Endocrinology* 1998;**139**:3296–305.

260. Kovacs G, Fine RN, Worgall S, Schaefer F, Hunziker EB, Skottner Lindun A, *et al.* Growth hormone prevents steroid-induced growth depression in health and uremia. *Kidney Int* 1991;**40**:1032–40.

261. Horber FF, Haymond MW. Human growth hormone prevents the protein catabolic side effects of prednisone in humans. *J Clin Invest* 1990;**86**:265–72.

262. Bennet WM, Haymond MW. Growth hormone and lean tissue catabolism during long-term glucocorticoid treatment. *Clin Endocrinol* 1992;**36**:161–4.

263. Schaefer F, Ritz E. Endocrine disorders in chronic renal failure. In: Cameron JS, Davison AM, Grünfeld J-P, Kerr DNS, Ritz E, editors. *Oxford Textbook of Clinical Nephrology.* Oxford: Oxford University Press; 1992. p. 1317–29.

264. Kaptein EM, Quion-Verde H, Chooljian CJ, Tang WW, Friedman PE, Rodriquez HJ, *et al.* The thyroid in end-stage renal disease. *Medicine (Baltimore)* 1988;**67**:187–97.

265. Hegedus L, Andersen JR, Poulsen LR, Perrild H, Holm B, Gundtoft E, *et al.* Thyroid gland volume

and serum concentrations of thyroid hormones in chronic renal failure. *Nephron* 1985;**40**:171–4.

266. Burke JR, El-Bishti MM, Maisey MN, Chantler C. Hypothyroidism in children with cystinosis. *Arch Dis Child* 1978;**53**:947–51.

267. McLean RH, Kennedy TL, Psoulpour M, Ratzan SK, Siegel NJ, Kauschansky A, *et al.* Hypothyroidism in the congenital nephrotic syndrome. *J Pediatr* 1982;**101**:72–5.

268. Koutras DA, Marketos SG, Rigopoulos GA, Malamos B. Iodine metabolism in chronic renal insufficiency. *Nephron* 1972;**9**:55–65.

269. Ramirez G, Jubiz W, Gutch CF, Bloomer HA, Siegler R, Kolff WJ. Thyroid abnormalities in renal failure. A study of 53 patients on chronic hemodialysis. *Ann Intern Med* 1973;**79**:500–4.

270. Robertson BF, Prestwich S, Ramirez G, O'Neill W, Jubiz W. The role of iodine in the pathogenesis of thyroid enlargement in rats with chronic renal failure. *Endocrinology* 1977;**101**:1272–5.

271. Kaptein EM, Feinstein EI, Nicoloff JT, Massry SG. Serum reverse triiodothyronine and thyroxine kinetics in patients with chronic renal failure. *J Clin Endocrinol Metab* 1983;**57**:181–9.

272. Kaptein EM, Kaptein JS, Chang EI, Egodage PM, Nicoloff JT, Massry SG. Thyroxine transfer and distribution in critical nonthyroidal illnesses, chronic renal failure, and chronic ethanol abuse. *J Clin Endocrinol Metabol* 1987;**65**:606–16.

273. Faber J, Heaf J, Kirkegaard C, Lumholtz IB, Siersbaek-Nielsen K, Kolendorf K, *et al.* Simultaneous turnover studies of thyroxine, 3,5,3'- and 3,3',5'-triiodothyronine, 3,5-, 3,3', and 3',5'-diiodothyronine, and 3'-monoiodothyronine in chronic renal failure. *J Clin Endocrinol Metabol* 1983;**56**:211–7.

274. Spector DA, Davis PJ, Helderman H, Bell B, Utiger RD. Thyroid function and metabolic state in chronic renal failure. *Ann Intern Med* 1976;**85**:724–30.

275. Kosowicz J, Malczewska B, Czekalski S. Serum reverse triiodothyronine (3,3',5'-L-triiodothyronine) in chronic renal failure. *Nephron* 1980;**26**:85–9.

276. De-Marchi S, Cecchin E, Villalta D, Tesio F. Serum reverse T3 assay for predicting glucose intolerance in uremic patients on dialysis therapy. *Clin Nephrol* 1987;**27**:189–98.

277. Bartalena L, Pacchiarotti A, Palla R, Antonangeli L, Mammoli C, Monzani F, *et al.* Lack of nocturnal serum thyrotropin (TSH) surge in patients with chronic renal failure undergoing maintenance hemofiltration: a case of central hypothyroidism. *Clin Nephrol* 1990;**34**:30–4.

278. Pasqualini T, Zantleifer D, Balzaretti M, Granillo E, Fainstein-Day P. Evidence of hypothalamic-pituitary thyroid abnormalities in children with end-stage renal disease. *J Pediatr* 1991;**118**:873–8.

279. Verger M, Verger C, Hatt-Magnien D, Perrone F. Relationship between thyroid hormones and nutrition in chronic failure. *Nephron* 1987;**45**:211–5.

280. Pagliacci MC, Pelicci G, Grignani F, Giammartino C, Fedeli L, Carobi C, *et al.* Thyroid function tests in patients undergoing maintenance dialysis: characterization of the 'low-T4 syndrome' in subjects on regular hemodialysis and continuous ambulatory peritoneal dialysis. *Nephron* 1987;**46**:225–30.

281. Robey C, Shreedhar K, Batuman V. Effects of chronic peritoneal dialysis on thyroid function tests. *Am J Kidney Dis* 1989;**13**:99–103.

282. Hardy MJ, Ragbeer SS, Nascimento L. Pituitary-thyroid function in chronic renal failure assessed by a highly sensitive thyrotropin assay. *J Clin Endocrinol Metab* 1988;**66**:233–6.

283. Beckett GJ, Henderson CJ, Elwes R, Seth J, Lambie AT. Thyroid status in patients with chronic renal failure. *Clin Nephrol* 1983;**19**:172–8.

284. Weissel M, Stummvoll HK, Kolbe H, Höfer R. Basal and TRH-stimulated thyroid and pituitary hormones in various degrees of renal insufficiency. *Acta Endocrinol (Copenh)* 1979;**90**:23–32.

285. Wheatley T, Clark PMS, Clark JDA, Holder R, Raggatt PR, Evans DB. Abnormalities of thyrotrophin (TSH) evening rise and pulsatile release in the haemodialysis patients: evidence for hypothalamic-pituitary changes in chronic renal failure. *Clin Endocrinol* 1989;**31**:39–50.

286. Rao MB, Bay WH, George JM, Hebert LA. Primary hypothyroidism in chronic renal failure. *Clin Nephrol* 1986;**25**:11–14.

287. Henneberg CM, Domenech JM, Montoya E. Thyrotrophin-releasing hormone responsiveness and degradation in children with chronic renal failure: effect of time of evolution. *Acta Endocrinol (Copenh)* 1982;**99**:508–16.

288. Weetman AP, Weightman DR, Scanlon MF. Impaired dopaminergic control of thyroid stimulating hormone secretion in chronic renal failure. *Clin Endocrinol (Oxf)* 1981;**15**:451–56.

289. Holliday MA, Chantler C. Metabolic and nutritional factors in children with renal insufficiency. *Kidney Int* 1978;**14**:306–12.

290. Lim VS, Henriquez C, Seo H, Refetoff S, Martino E. Thyroid function in a uremic rat model. *J Clin Invest* 1980;**66**:946–54.

291. Kinlaw WB, Schwartz HL, Mariash CN, Bingham C, Carr FE, Oppenheimer JH. Hepatic messenger ribonucleic acid activity profiles in experimental azotemia in the rat. Relationship to food intake and thyroid function. *J Clin Invest* 1984;**74**:1934–41.

292. Oppenheimer JH. Thyroid hormone action at the nuclear level. *Ann Intern Med* 1985;**102**:374–84.

293. Williams GR, Franklyn JA, Neuberger JM, Sheppard MC. Thyroid hormone receptor expression in the 'sick euthyroid' syndrome. *Lancet* 1989;**2**:1477–81.

294. Lim VS, Zavala DC, Flanigan MJ, Freeman RM. Blunted peripheral tissue responsiveness to thyroid hormone in uremic patients. *Kidney Int* 1987;**31**:808–14.

295. Lim VS, Flanigan MJ, Zavala DC, Freeman RM. Protective adaptation of low serum tri-iodothyronine in patients with chronic renal failure. *Kidney Int* 1985;**28**:541–9.

296. Spaulding SW, Chopra IJ, Sherwin RS, Lyall SS. Effect of caloric restriction and dietary composition on serum T_3 and reverse T_3 in man. *J Clin Endocrinol Metab* 1976;**42**:197–200.

297. van Leusen R, Meinders AE. Cyclical changes in serum thyroid hormone concentrations related to hemodialysis: movement of hormone into and out of the extravascular space as a possible mechanism. *Clin Nephrol* 1982;**18**:193–9.

298. Sharp NA, Devlin JT, Rimmer JM. Renal failure obfuscates the diagnosis of Cushing's disease. *JAMA* 1986;**256**:2564–5.

299. Ramirez G, Gomez-Sanchez C, Meikle WA, Jubiz W. Evaluation of the hypothalamic hypophyseal adrenal axis in patients receiving long-term hemodialysis. *Arch Intern Med* 1982;**142**:1448–52.

300. Zager PG, Frey HJ, Gerdes BG. Plasma 18-hydroxycorticosterone during continuous ambulatory peritoneal dialysis. *J Lab Clin Med* 1983;**102**:604–12.

301. Luger A, Lang I, Kovarik J, Stummvoll HK, Templ H. Abnormalities in the hypothalamic-pituitary-adrenocortical axis in patients with chronic renal failure. *Am J Kidney Dis* 1987; **9**:51–4.

302. Ramirez G, Brueggemeyer C, Ganguly A. Counterregulatory hormonal response to insulin-induced hypoglycemia in patients on chronic hemodialysis. *Nephron* 1988;**49**:231–6.

303. Wallace EZ, Rosman P, Toshav N, Sacerdote A, Balthazar A. Pituitary-adrenocortical function in chronic renal failure: studies of episodic secretion of cortisol and dexamethasone suppressibility. *J Clin Endocrinol Metab* 1980; **50**:46–51.

304. Betts PR, Hose PM, Morris R. Serum cortisol concentrations in children with chronic renal insufficiency. *Arch Dis Child* 1975;**50**:245–7.

305. Ferraris JR, Ramirez JA, Goldberg V, Rivarola MA. Glucocorticoids and adrenal androgens in children with end-stage renal disease. *Acta Endocrinol (Copenh)* 1991;**124**:245–50.

306. Cooke CR, Whelton PK, Moore MA, Caputo RA, Bledsoe T, Walker WG. Dissociation of the diurnal variation of aldosterone and cortisol in anephric patients. *Kidney Int* 1979;**15**:669–75.

307. Deck KA, Baur P, Hillen H. Plasma clearance of cortisol as a function of plasma cortisol levels in normal and obese persons and in patients with uremia or cirrhosis of the liver. *Acta Endocrinol (Copenh)* 1979;**91**:122–33.

308. McDonald WJ, Golper TA, Mass RD, Kendall JW, Porter GA, Girard DE, *et al.* Adreno-corticotropin-cortisol axis abnormalities in hemodialysis patients. *J Clin Endocrinol Metab* 1979;**48**:92–5.

309. Grekas D, Tourkantonis A, Pharmakiotis A. Adrenal responsiveness during and after intermittent haemodialysis. *Clin Exp Dial Apheresis* 1983;**7**:197–205.

310. Zager PG, Spalding CT, Frey HJ, Brittenham MC. Low dose adrenocorticotropin infusion in continuous ambulatory peritoneal dialysis patients. *J Clin Endocrinol Metab* 1985;**61**:1205–10.

311. Ramirez G, Ganguly A, Brueggemeyer C, Gomez-Sanchez C. Aldosterone response to insulin-induced hypoglycemia in hemodialysis patients. *Am J Nephrol* 1989;**9**:215–21.

312. Williams GH, Bailey GL, Hampers CL, Lauler DP, Merrill JP, Underwood RH, *et al.* Studies on the metabolism of aldosterone in chronic renal failure and anephric man. *Kidney Int* 1973;**4**: 280–8.

313. Rodger RSC, Watson MJ, Sellars L, Wilkinson R, Ward MK, Kerr DNS. Hypothalamic-pituitary-adrenocortical suppression and recovery in renal transplant patients returning to maintenance dialysis. *Q J Med* 1986;**61**:1039–46.

314. van Coevorden A, Stolear JC, Dhaene M, van Herweghem JL, Mockel J. Effect of chronic oral testosterone undecanoate administration on the pituitary-testicular axis of hemodialyzed male patients. *Clin Nephrol* 1986;**26**:48–54.

315. Mastrogiacomo I, de Besi L, Zucchetta P, Serafini E, la Greca G, Gasparoto ML, *et al.* Male hypogonadism of uremic patients on hemodialysis. *Arch Androl* 1988;**20**:171–5.

316. Siamopoulos KC, Eleftheriades EG, Pappas M, Sferopoulos G, Tsolas O. Ovine corticotropin-releasing hormone stimulation test in patients with chronic renal failure: pharmacokinetic properties, and plasma adrenocorticotropic hormone and serum cortisol responses. *Horm Res* 1988;**30**:17–21.

317. Rosman PM, Farag A, Peckham R, Benn R, Tito J, Bacci V, *et al.* Pituitary-adrenocortical function in chronic renal failure: blunted suppression and early escape of plasma cortisol levels after intravenous dexamethasone. *J Clin Endocrinol Metab* 1982;**54**:528–33.

318. Kawai S, Ichikawa Y, Homma M. Differences in metabolic properties among cortisol, prednisolone, and dexamethasone in liver and renal diseases: accelerated metabolism of dexamethasone in renal failure. *J Clin Endocrinol Metab* 1985;**60**:848–54.

319. Defronzo RA, Tobin J, Andres R. The glucose clamp technique. A method or the quantification of beta cell sensitivity to glucose and of tissue sensitivity to insulin. *Am J Physiol* 1979;**237**: 214–23.

320. Katz AI, Rubenstein AH. Metabolism of proinsulin, insulin, and C-peptide in the rat. *J Clin Invest* 1973;**52**:1113–21.

321. Hampers CL, Soeldner JS, Doak PB, Merrill JP. Effect of chronic renal failure and hemodialysis on carbohydrate metabolism. *J Clin Invest* 1966;**45**:1719–31.

322. Smith WG, Hanning I, Johnston DG, Brown CB. Pancreatic beta-cell function in CAPD. *Nephrol Dial Transplant* 1988;**3**:448–52.

323. Lowrie EG, Soeldner JS, Hamoers CL, Merril JP. Glucose metabolism and insulin secretion in uremic, prediabetic, and normal subjects. *J Lab Clin Med* 1970;**76**:603–15.

324. Spitz IM, Rubinstein AH, Behrson I, Abrahams C, Lowry C. Carbohydrate metabolism in renal disease. *Q J Med* 1970;**39**:201–26.

325. Schmitz O. Effects of physiologic and supra-physiologic hyperglycemia on early and late-phase insulin secretion in chronically dialyzed uremic patients. *Acta Endocrinol (Copenh)* 1989;**121**:251–8.

326. Nakamura Y, Yoshida T, Kajiyama S, Kitagawa Y, Kanatsuna T, Kondo M. Insulin release from column-perifused isolated islets of uremic rats. *Nephron* 1985;**40**:467–9.

327. Defronzo RA, Tobin JD, Rowe JW, Andres R. Glucose intolerance in uremia. *J Clin Invest* 1978;**62**:425–35.

328. Alvestrand A, Mujagic M, Wajngot A, Efendic S. Glucose intolerance in uremic patients: the relative contributions of impaired beta-cell function and insulin resistance. *Clin Nephrol* 1989;**31**:175–83.

329. Mak RH, Bettinelli A, Turner C, Haycock GB, Chantler C. The influence of hyperparathyroidism on glucose metabolism in uremia. *J Clin Endocrinol Metab* 1985;**60**:229–33.

330. Mak RHK, Turner C, Haycock GB, Chantler C. Secondary hyperparathyroidism and glucose intolerance in children with uremia. *Kidney Int* 1983;**24**:128–33.

331. Fadda GZ, Akmal M, Premdas FH, Lipson LG, Massry SG. Insulin release from pancreatic islets: effects of CRF and excess PTH. *Kidney Int* 1988;**33**:1066–72.

332. Fadda GZ, Akmal M, Soliman AR, Lipson LG, Massry SG. Correction of glucose intolerance and the impaired insulin release of chronic renal failure by verapamil. *Kidney Int* 1989;**36**:773–9.

333. Defronzo RA, Alvestrand A. Glucose intolerance in uremia: site and mechanism. *Am J Clin Nutr* 1980;**33**:1438–45.

334. Mak RH, Haycock GB, Chantler C. Glucose intolerance in children with chronic renal failure. *Kidney Int* 1983;**24**:22–6.

335. Kalhan SC, Ricanati ES, Tserng KY, Savin SM. Glucose turnover in chronic uremia: increased recycling with diminished oxidation of glucose. *Metabolism* 1983;**32**:1155–62.

336. Schmitz O. Peripheral and hepatic resistance to insulin and hepatic resistance to glucagon in uraemic subjects. *Acta Endocrinol (Copenh)* 1988;**118**:125–34.

337. Westervelt FB, Schreiner GE. The carbohydrate intolerance of uremic patients. *Ann Intern Med* 1962;**57**:266–75.

338. Deferrari G, Garibotto G, Robaudo C, Lutman M, Viviani G, Sala R, *et al*. Glucose interorgan exchange in chronic renal failure. *Kidney Int* 1983;**24**:115–20.

339. Taylor R, Heaton A, Hetherington CS, Alberti KG. Adipocyte insulin binding and insulin action in chronic renal failure before and during continuous ambulatory peritoneal dialysis. *Metabolism* 1986;**35**:430–5.

340. Weisinger JR, Contreras NE, Cajias J, Bellorin-Font E, Amair P, Guitierrez L, *et al*. Insulin binding and glycolytic activity in erythrocytes from dialyzed and nondialyzed uremic patients. *Nephron* 1988;**48**:190–6.

341. Pedersen O, Schmitz O, Hjollund E, Richelsen B, Hansen HE. Postbinding defects of insulin action in human adipocytes from uremic patients. *Kidney Int* 1985;**27**:780–4.

342. Schmitz O, Alberti KGM, Christensen NJ. Aspects of glucose homeostasis in uremia as assessed by the hyperinsulinemic clamp technique. *Metabolism* 1985;**34**:465–73.

343. Maloff BL, McCaleb M, Lockwood DH. Cellular basis of insulin resistance in chronic uremia. *Am J Physiol* 1983;**245**:178–84.

344. Bak JF, Schmitz O, Sorensen SS, Frokjaer J, Kjaer T, Pedersen O. Activity of insulin receptor kinase and glycogen synthase in skeletal muscle from patients with chronic renal failure. *Acta Endocrinol (Copenh)* 1989;**121**:744–50.

345. Schmitz O, Arnfred J, Orskov L, Nielsen OH, Orskov H, Posborg V. Influence of hyperglycemia on glucose uptake and hepatic glucose production in non-dialyzed uremic patients. *Clin Nephrol* 1988;**30**:27–34.

346. Guarnieri G, Toigo G, de Marchi S, Situlin R, Campanacci L. Muscle hexokinase and phosphofructokinase activity in chronically uremic patients. In: Giordano C, Friedman EA, editors. Uremia. Milan: *Wichtig*; 1981. p. 278.

347. Mak RH. Insulin resistance in uremia: effect of dialysis modality. *Pediatr Res* 1996;**40**:304–8.

348. Mak RH, Turner C, Thompson T, Haycock G, Chantler C. The effect of a low protein diet with amino acid/keto acid supplements on glucose metabolism in children with uremia. *J Clin Endocrinol Metab* 1986;**63**:985–9.

349. Gin H, Aparicio M, Potaux L, de-Precigout V, Bouchet JL, Aubertin J. Low protein and low phosphorus diet in patients with chronic renal

failure: influence on glucose tolerance and tissue insulin sensitivity. *Metabolism* 1987;**36**:1080–5.

350. Hörl WH, Haag-Weber M, Georgopoulos A, Block LH. Physicochemical characterization of a polypeptide present in uremic serum that inhibits the biological activity of polymorphonuclear cells. *Proc Natl Acad Sci U S A* 1990;**87**:6353–7.

351. Dzúrik R, Hupková V, Cernacek P, Valovicova E, Niederland TR, Mayskova A, *et al.* The isolation of an inhibitor of glucose utilization from the serum of uraemic subjects. *Clin Chim Acta* 1973;**46**:77–83.

352. McCaleb ML, Wish JB, Lockwood DH. Insulin resistance in chronic renal failure. *Endocr Res* 1985;**11**:113–25.

353. Mak RHK, Chang S, Xie WW. 1,25 Dihydroxycholecalciferol reverses insulin resistance and hypertension in the uremic rat. *Pediatr Res* 1991;**29**:346A.

354. Mak RH. Effect of recombinant human erythropoietin on insulin, amino acid, and lipid metabolism in uremia. *J Pediatr* 1996;**129**:97–104.

355. Jaspan JB, Rubenstein AH. Circulating glucagon. Plasma profiles and metabolism in health and disease. *Diabetes* 1977;**26**:887–902.

356. Sherwin RS, Bastl C, Finkelstein FO, Fisher M, Black H, Hendler R, et al. Influence of uremia and hemodialysis on the turnover and metabolic effects of glucagon. *J Clin Invest* 1976;**57**:722–31.

357. Dighe RR, Rojas FJ, Birnbaumer L, Garber AJ. Glucagon-stimulable adenylyl cyclase in rat liver. Effects of chronic uremia and intermittent glucagon administration. *J Clin Invest* 1984; **73**:1004–12.

358. del Prato S, Castellino P, Simonson DC, Defronzo RA. Hyperglucagonemia and insulin-mediated glucose metabolism. *J Clin Invest* 1987;**79**:547–56.

359. Heaton A, Johnston DG, Burrin JM, Orskov H, Ward MK, Alberti KGM, *et al.* Carbohydrate and lipid metabolism during continuous ambulatory dialysis (CAPD): the effect of a single dialysis cycle. *Clin Sci* 1983;**65**:539–45.

360. Armstrong VW, Creutzfeldt W, Ebert R, Fuchs C, Hilgers R, Scheler F. Effect of dialysate glucose load on plasma glucose and glucoregulatory hormones in CAPD patients. *Nephron* 1985;**39**:141–5.

361. Lindholm B, Karlander SG. Glucose tolerance in patients undergoing continuous ambulatory peritoneal dialysis. *Acta Med Scand* 1986; **220**:477–83.

362. Heaton A, Taylor R, Johnston DG, Ward MK, Wilkinson R, Alberti KG. Hepatic and peripheral insulin action in chronic renal failure before and during continuous ambulatory peritoneal dialysis. *Clin Sci* 1989;**77**:383–8.

363. Cobo A, Lopez JM, Carbajo E, Santos F, Alvarez J, Fernandez M, *et al.* Growth plate cartilage formation and resorption are differentially depressed in growth retarded uremic rats. *J Am Soc Nephrol* 1999;**10**:971–9.

364. Cobo A, Carbajo E, Santos F, Garcia E, Lopez JM. Morphometry of uremic rat growth plate. *Miner Electrolyte Metab* 1996;**22**:192–5.

365. Mehls O, Ritz E, Hunziker EB, Eggli P, Heinrich U, Zapf J. Improvement of growth and food utilization by human recombinant growth hormone in uremia. *Kidney Int* 1988;**33**:45–52.

366. Hanna JD, Santos F, Foreman JW, Chan JC, Han VK. Insulin-like growth factor-I gene expression in the tibial epiphyseal growth plate of growth hormone-treated uremic rats. *Kidney Int* 1995;**47**:1374–82.

367. Alvarez J, Balbin M, Fernandez M, Lopez JM. Collagen metabolism is markedly altered in the hypertrophic cartilage of growth plates from rats with growth impairment secondary to chronic renal failure. *J Bone Miner Res* 2001;**16**:511–24.

368. Sanchez CP, Salusky IB, Kuizon BD, Abdella P, Juppner H, Goodman WG. Growth of long bones in renal failure: roles of hyperparathyroidism, growth hormone and calcitriol. *Kidney Int* 1998;**54**:1879–87.

369. Sanchez CP, Kuizon BD, Abdella PA, Juppner H, Salusky IB, Goodman WG. Impaired growth, delayed ossification, and reduced osteoclastic activity in the growth plate of calcium-supplemented rats with renal failure. *Endocrinology* 2000;**141**:1536–44.

370. Juppner H. Role of parathyroid hormone-related peptide and Indian hedgehog in skeletal development. *Pediatr Nephrol* 2000;**14**:606–11.

371. Karaplis AC, Luz A, Glowacki J, Bronson RT, Tybulewicz VL, Kronenberg HM, *et al.* Lethal skeletal dysplasia from targeted disruption of the parathyroid hormone-related peptide gene. *Genes Dev* 1994;**8**:277–89.

372. Lanske B, Karaplis AC, Lee K, Luz A, Vortkamp A, Pirro A, *et al.* PTH/PTHrP receptor in early development and Indian hedgehog-regulated bone growth. *Science* 1996;**273**:663–6.

373. Weir EC, Philbrick WM, Amling M, Neff LA, Baron R, Broadus AE. Targeted overexpression of parathyroid hormone-related peptide in chondrocytes causes chondrodysplasia and delayed endochondral bone formation. *Proc Natl Acad Sci U S A* 1996;**93**:10240–5.

374. Schipani E, Kruse K, Juppner H. A constitutively active mutant PTH-PTHrP receptor in Jansen-type metaphyseal chondrodysplasia. *Science* 1995;**268**:98–100.

375. Jobert AS, Zhang P, Couvineau A, Bonaventure J, Roume J, Le Merrer M, *et al.* Absence of functional receptors for parathyroid hormone and parathyroid hormone-related peptide in Blomstrand chondrodysplasia. *J Clin Invest* 1998;**102**:34–40.

376. Coen G, Mazzaferro S, Ballanti P, Sardella D, Chicca S, Manni M, *et al*. Renal bone disease in 76 patients with varying degrees of predialysis chronic renal failure: a cross-sectional study. *Nephrol Dial Transplant* 1996;**11**:813–19.

377. Urena P, Mannstadt M, Hruby M, Ferreira A, Schmitt F, Silve C, *et al*. Parathyroidectomy does not prevent the renal PTH/PTHrP receptor down-regulation in uremic rats. *Kidney Int* 1995;**47**:1797–805.

378. Urena P, Ferreira A, Morieux C, Drueke T, de Vernejoul MC. PTH/PTHrP receptor mRNA is down-regulated in epiphyseal cartilage growth plate of uraemic rats. *Nephrol Dial Transplant* 1996;**11**:2008–16.

379. Urena P, Kubrusly M, Mannstadt M, Hruby M, Trinh MM, Silve C, *et al*. The renal PTH/PTHrP receptor is down-regulated in rats with chronic renal failure. *Kidney Int* 1994;**45**:605–11.

380. Picton ML, Moore PR, Mawer EB, Houghton D, Freemont AJ, Hutchison AJ, *et al*. Down-regulation of human osteoblast PTH/PTHrP receptor mRNA in end-stage renal failure. *Kidney Int* 2000;**58**:1440–9.

381. Edmondson SR, Baker NL, Oh J, Kovacs G, Werther GA, Mehls O. Growth hormone receptor abundance in tibial growth plates of uremic rats: GH/IGF-I treatment. *Kidney Int* 2000;**58**:62–70.

382. Green J, Maor G. Effect of metabolic acidosis on the growth hormone/IGF-I endocrine axis in skeletal growth centers. *Kidney Int* 2000;**57**:2258–67.

383. Saggese G, Federico G, Cinquanta L. *In vitro* effects of growth hormone and other hormones on chondrocytes and osteoblast-like cells. *Acta Paediatr Suppl* 1993;**391**:54–9.

384. Scharla SH, Strong DD, Mohan S, Baylink DJ, Linkhart TA. 1,25-Dihydroxyvitamin D3 differentially regulates the production of insulin-like growth factor I (IGF-I) and IGF-binding protein-4 in mouse osteoblasts. *Endocrinology* 1991;**129**:3139–46.

385. Silbermann M, Mirsky N, Levitan S, Weisman Y. The effect of 1,25-dihydroxyvitamin D3 on cartilage growth in neonatal mice. *Metab Bone Dis Relat Res* 1983;**4**:337–45.

386. Weinreb M, Jr., Gazit E, Weinreb MM. Mandibular growth and histologic changes in condylar cartilage of rats intoxicated with vitamin D3 or 1,25(OH)$_2$D$_3$ and pair-fed (undernourished) rats. *J Dent Res* 1986;**65**:1449–52.

387. Silbermann M, von der Mark K, Mirsky N, van Menxel M, Lewinson D. Effects of increased doses of 1,25 dihydroxyvitamin D$_3$ on matrix and DNA synthesis in condylar cartilage of suckling mice. *Calcif Tissue Int* 1987;**41**:95–104.

388. Kainer G, Nakano M, Massie FS Jr, Foreman JW, Chan JC. Hypercalciuria due to combined growth hormone and calcitriol therapy in uremia: effects of growth hormone on mineral homeostasis in 75% nephrectomized weanling rats. *Pediatr Res* 1991;**30**:528–33.

389. Klaus G, Weber L, Rodriguez J, Fernandez P, Klein T, Grulich-Henn J, *et al*. Interaction of IGF-I and 1 alpha, 25(OH)$_2$D$_3$ on receptor expression and growth stimulation in rat growth plate chondrocytes. *Kidney Int* 1998;**53**:1152–61.

390 Baron J, Klein KO, Colli MJ, Yanovski JA, Novosad JA, Bacher JD, *et al*. Catch-up growth after glucocorticoid excess: a mechanism intrinsic to the growth plate. *Endocrinology* 1994;**135**:1367–71.

391. Silbermann M, Maor G. Mechanisms of glucocorticoid-induced growth retardation: impairment of cartilage mineralization. *Acta Anat (Basel)* 1978;**101**:140–9.

392. Heinrichs C, Yanovski JA, Roth AH, Yu YM, Domene HM, Yano K, *et al*. Dexamethasone increases growth hormone receptor messenger ribonucleic acid levels in liver and growth plate. *Endocrinology* 1994;**135**:1113–18.

393. Klaus G, Jux C, Fernandez P, Rodriguez J, Himmele R, Mehls O. Suppression of growth plate chondrocyte proliferation by cortico-steroids. *Pediatr Nephrol* 2000;**14**:612–15.

394. Silvestrini G, Ballanti P, Patacchioli FR, Mocetti P, Di Grezia R, Wedard BM, *et al*. Evaluation of apoptosis and the glucocorticoid receptor in the cartilage growth plate and metaphyseal bone cells of rats after high-dose treatment with corticosterone. *Bone* 2000;**26**:33–42.

395. Strife CF, Quinlan M, Mears K, Davey ML, Clardy C. Improved growth of three uremic children by nocturnal nasogastric feedings. *Am J Dis Child* 1986;**140**:438–43.

396. Rodriguez-Soriano J, Arant BS, Brodehl J, Norman ME. Fluid and electrolyte imbalances in children with chronic renal failure. *Am J Kidney Dis* 1986;**7**:268–9.

397. Trachtman H, Hackney P, Tejani A. Pediatric hemodialysis: a decade's (1974–1984) perspective. *Kidney Int* 1986;**30**:15–22.

398. Fennell RS (III), Orak JK, Hudson T, Garin EH, Iravani A, Van Deusen WJ, *et al*. Growth in children with various therapies for end-stage renal disease. *Am J Dis Child* 1984;**138**:28–31.

399. Chantler C, Donckerwolcke RA, Brunner FP, Gurland HJ, Jacobs C, Selwood NH, *et al*. Combined report on regular dialysis and transplantation of children in Europe 1976. In: Robinson BHB, Hawkins JB, Vereerstraete P, editors. *Dialysis transplantation nephrology*. Vol. 14. Tunbridge Wells: Pitman Medical Publications; 1977. p. 70–126.

400. Anonymous. Continuous ambulatory and continuous cycling peritoneal dialysis in children. A report of the Southwest Pediatric Nephrology Study Group. *Kidney Int* 1985;**27**:558–64.

401. Potter DE, Luis E, San, Wipfler JE, Portale AA. Comparison of continuous ambulatory peritoneal dialysis and hemodialysis in children. *Kidney Int* 1986;**30**:11–14.

402. Fine RN, Mehls O. CAPD/CCPD in children: four years' experience. *Kidney Int* 1986;**30**:7–10.

403. von Lilien T, Gilli G, Salusky IB. Growth in children undergoing continuous ambulatory or cycling peritoneal dialysis. In: Schärer K, editor. *Pediatric and adolescent endocrinology.* Vol. 20. Basel: Karger; 1989. p. 27–35.

404. Kohaut EC, Alexander SR, Mehls O. The management of the infant on CAPD. In: Fine RN, Schärer K, Mehls O, editors. *CAPD in children.* Berlin: Springer; 1985. p. 97–105.

405. Ingelfinger JR, Grupe WE, Harmon WE, Fernbach SK, Levey RH. Growth acceleration following renal transplantation in children less than 7 years of age. *Pediatrics* 1981;**68**:255–9.

406. Ruder H, Strehlau J, Schaefer F, Gretz N, Müller-Wiefel DE, Bonzel KE, et al. Low-dose cyclosporin A therapy in cadaver renal transplantation in children. *Transplant Int* 1989; **2**:203–8.

407. Reisman L, Lieberman KV, Burrows L, Schanzer H. Follow-up of cyclosporine-treated pediatric renal allograft recipients after cessation of prednisone. *Transplantation* 1990;**49**:76–80.

408. Broyer M, Guest G, Gagnadoux M. Growth rate in children receiving alternate-day corticosteroid treatment after kidney transplantation. *J Pediatr* 1992;**120**:721–5.

409. Kaiser BA, Polinsky MS, Palmer JA, Dunn S, Mochon M, Flynn JT, et al. Growth after conversion to alternate-day corticosteroids in children with renal transplants: a single-center study. *Pediatr Nephrol* 1994;**8**:320–5.

410. Hokken-Koelega AC, Van Zaal MA, de Ridder MA, Wilff ED, de Jong MC, Donckerwolcke RA, et al. Growth after renal transplantation in prepubertal children: impact of various treatment modalities. *Pediatr Res* 1994;**35**:367–71.

411. Pennisi AJ, Costin G, Phillips LS, Uittenbogaart C, Ettenger RB, Malekzadeh MH, et al. Linear growth in long-term renal allograft recipients. *Clin Nephrol* 1977;**8**:415–21.

412. So SKS, Chang P, Najaran JS, Mauer SM, Simmons RL, Nevins TE. Growth and development in infants after renal transplantation. *J Pediatr* 1987;**110**:343–50.

413. Tejani A, Fine R, Alexander S, Harmon W, Stablein D. Factors predictive of sustained growth in children after renal transplantation. The North American Pediatric Renal Transplant Cooperative Study. *J Pediatr* 1993;**122**:397–402.

414. Tejani A, Cortes L, Sullivan EK. A longitudinal study of the natural history of growth post-transplantation. *Kidney Int Suppl* 1996;**53**: 103–8.

415. DeShazo CV, Simmons RL, Berstein SM, DeShazo MM, Willmert J, Kjellstrand CM, et al. Results of renal transplantation in 100 children. *Surgery* 1974;**76**:461–3.

416. Sarna S, Hoppu K, Neuvonen PJ, Laine J, Holmberg C. Methylprednisolone exposure, rather than dose, predicts adrenal suppression and growth inhibition in children with liver and renal transplantation. *J Clin Endocrinol Metab* 1997;**82**:75–7.

417. Jabs K, Sullivan EK, Avner ED, Harmon WE. Alternate-day steroid dosing improves growth without affecting graft survival or long-term graft function. A report of the North American Pediatric Renal Transplant Cooperative Study. *Transplantation* 1996;**61**:31–6.

418. Klare B, Strom TM, Hahn H, Engelsberger I, Meusel E, Illner W, et al. Remarkable long-term prognosis and excellent growth in kidney-transplant children under cyclosporine monotherapy. *Transplant Proc* 1991;**23**:1013–17.

419. Chao SM, Jones CL, Powell HR, Johnstone L, Francis DM, Becker GJ, et al. Triple immunosuppression with subsequent prednisolone withdrawal: 6 years' experience in paediatric renal allograft recipients. *Pediatr Nephrol* 1994;**8**:62–9.

420. Ingulli E, Sharma V, Singh A, Suthanthiran M, Tejani A. Steroid withdrawal, rejection and the mixed lymphocyte reaction in children after renal transplantation. *Kidney Int Suppl* 1993;**43**:36–9.

421. Ferraris J, Day PF, Gutman R, Granillo E, Ramirez J, Ruiz S, et al. Effect of therapy with a new glucocorticoid, deflazacort, on linear growth and growth hormone secretion after renal transplantation. *J Pediatr* 1992;**121**:809–13.

422. Rees L, Rigden SPA, Ward G, Preece MA. Treatment of short stature in renal disease with recombinant human growth hormone. *Arch Dis Child* 1990;**65**:856–60.

423. Koch VH, Lippe BM, Nelson PA, Boechat MI, Sherman BM, Fine RN. Accelerated growth after recombinant human growth hormone treatment of children with chronic renal failure. *J Pediatr* 1989;**115**:365–71.

424. Tönshoff B, Dietz M, Haffner D, Tönshoff C, Stöver B, Mehls O. Effects of two years growth hormone treatment in short children with renal disease. *Acta Paediatr Scand Suppl* 1991;**379**:33–41.

425. Fine RN, Kohaut EC, Brown D, Perlman AJ. Growth after recombinant human growth hormone treatment in children with chronic renal failure: report of a multicenter randomized double-blind placebo-controlled study. Genentech Cooperative Study Group. *J Pediatr* 1994; **124**:374–82.

426. Fine RN, Kohaut E, Brown D, Kuntze J, Attie KM. Long-term treatment of growth retarded children with chronic renal insufficiency, with

recombinant human growth hormone. *Kidney Int* 1996;**49**:781–5.

427. Hokken-Koelega A, Mulder P, de Jong R, Lilien M, Donckerwolcke R, Groothoff J. Long-term effects of growth hormone treatment on growth and puberty in patients with chronic renal insufficiency. *Pediatr Nephrol* 2000;**14**:701–6.

428. Wühl E, Haffner D, Tönshoff B, Mehls O. Predictors of growth response to rhGH in short children before and after renal transplantation. German Study Group for Growth Hormone Treatment in Chronic Renal Failure. *Kidney Int* 1993;**43**:76–82.

429. Berard E, Crosnier H, Six-Beneton A, Chevallier T, Cochat P, Broyer M. Recombinant human growth hormone treatment of children on hemodialysis. French Society of Pediatric Nephrology. *Pediatr Nephrol* 1998;**12**:304–10.

430. Schaefer F, Wühl E, Haffner D, Mehls O, German Study Group for Growth Hormone Treatment in Chronic Renal Failure. Stimulation of growth hormone in children undergoing peritoneal or hemodialysis treatment. *Adv Perit Dial* 1994;**10**:321–6.

431. Wühl E, Haffner D, Gretz N, Offner G, van't Hoff WG, Broyer M, *et al.* for the The European Study Group on Growth Hormone Treatment in Short Children with Nephropathic Cystinosis. Treatment with recombinant human growth hormone in short children with nephropathic cystinosis: no evidence for increased deterioration rate of renal function. *Pediatr Res* 1998; **43**:484–8.

432. van Es A. Growth hormone treatment in short children with chronic renal failure and after renal transplantation: combined data from European clinical trials. The European Study Group. *Acta Paediatr Scand Suppl* 1991;**379**:42–8.

433. Johannson GJ. Treatment with Genotropin in short children with chronic renal failure, either before active replacement therapy or with functioning renal transplants. An interim report on five European studies. *Acta Paediatr Scand Suppl* 1990;**370**:36–42.

434. Fine RN, Yadin O, Nelson PA, Pyke-Grimm K, Boechat MI, Lippe BH, *et al.* Recombinant human growth hormone treatment of children following renal transplantation. *Pediatr Nephrol* 1991;**5**:147–51.

435. van Dop C, Jabs KL, Donohue PA, Bock GH, Fivush BA, Harmon WE. Accelerated growth rates in children treated with growth hormone after renal transplantation. *J Pediatr* 1992; **120**:244–50.

436. Hokken-Koelega AC, Stijnen T, de Jong RC, Donckerwolcke RA, Groothoff JW, Wolff ED, et al. A placebo-controlled, double-blind trial of growth hormone treatment in prepubertal children after renal transplant. *Kidney Int Suppl* 1996;**53**:128–34.

437. Guest G, Berard E, Crosnier H, Chevallier T, Rappaport R, Broyer M. Effects of growth hormone in short children after renal transplantation. *Pediatr Nephrol* 1998;**12**:437–46.

438. Haffner D, Wühl E, Tönshoff B, Mehls O. Growth hormone treatment in short children: 5-year experience German Study Group for Growth Hormone Treatment in Chronic Renal Failure. *Nephrol Dial Transplant* 1994;**9**:960–1.

439. Abitbol CL, Zilleruelo G, Montane B, Strauss J. Growth of uremic infants on forced feeding regimens. *Pediatr Nephrol* 1993;**7**:173–7.

440. Mehls O, Berg U, Broyer M, Rizzoni G. Chronic renal failure and growth hormone treatment: review of the literature and experience in KIGS. In: Ranke MB, Wilton P, editors. *Growth hormone therapy in KIGS – 10 years experience.* 1st ed. Heidelberg: Barth; 1999. p. 327–40.

441. Rees L, Ward G, Rigden SPA. Growth over 10 years following a 1-year trial of growth hormone therapy. *Pediatr Nephrol* 2000;**14**:309–14.

442. Fine RN, Sullivan EK, Tejani A. The impact of recombinant human growth hormone treatment on final adult height. *Pediatr Nephrol* 2000; **14**:679–81.

443. Janssen F, Van Damme-Lombaerts R, Van Dyck M, Hall M, Schurmans T, Herman J, *et al.* Impact of growth hormone treatment on a Belgian population of short children with renal allografts. *Pediatr Transplant* 1997;**1**:190–6.

444. Haffner D, Schaefer F. Does recombinant growth hormone improve adult height in children with chronic renal failure? *Semin Nephrol* 2001; **21**:490–7.

445. Hokken-Koelega AC, Stijnen T, de Jong MC, Donckerwolcke RA, De Muinck Keizer-Schrama SM. Double blind trial comparing the effects of two doses of growth hormone in prepubertal patients with chronic renal insufficiency. *J Clin Endocrinol Metab* 1994;**79**:1185–90.

446. Hokken-Koelega AC, Stijnen T, de Ridder MA, de Munick Keizer-Schrama SM, Wolff ED, de Jong MC, *et al.* Growth hormone treatment in growth-retarded adolescents after renal transplant. *Lancet* 1994;**343**:1313–7.

447. Fine RN. Recombinant human growth hormone (rhGH) treatment in children with chronic renal failure (CRF): long-term (one to three years) outcome. *Pediatr Nephrol* 1991;**5**:477–81.

448. Fine RN, Brown DF, Kuntze J, Wooster P, Kohaut EE. Growth after discontinuation of recombinant human growth hormone therapy in children with chronic renal failure. *J Pediatr* 1996;**129**:883–91.

449. Tönshoff B, Heinrich U, Mehls O. How safe is the treatment of uraemic children with recombinant human growth hormone? *Pediatr Nephrol* 1991;**5**:454–60.

450. Haffner D, Nissel R, Wühl E, Schaefer F, Bettendorf M, Tönshoff B, *et al.* Metabolic

effects of long-term growth hormone treatment in prepubertal children with chronic renal failure and after kidney transplantation. *Pediatr Res* 1997;**43**:209–15.

451. Robert JJ, Tete MJ, Guest G, Gagnadoux MF, Niaudet P, Broyer M. Diabetes mellitus in patients with infantile cystinosis after renal transplantation. *Pediatr Nephrol* 1999;**13**:524–9.

452. Filler G, Amendt P, von Bredow MA, Rohde W, Ehrich JHH. Slowly deteriorating insulin secretion and C-peptide production characterizes diabetes mellitus in infantile cystinosis. *Eur J Pediatr* 1998;**157**:738–42.

453. Filler G, Franke D, Amendt P, Ehrich JH. Reversible diabetes mellitus during growth hormone therapy in chronic renal failure. *Pediatr Nephrol* 1998;**12**:405–7.

454. Stefanidis CP, Papathanassiou A, Michelis K, Theodoridis X, Papachristou F, Sotiriou J. Diabetes mellitus after therapy with recombinant human growth hormone. *Br J Clin Pract Suppl* 1996;**85**:66–7.

455. Cutfield WS, Wilton P, Bennmarker H, Albertsson-Wikland K, Chatelain P, Ranke MB, *et al.* Incidence of diabetes mellitus and impaired glucose tolerance in children and adolescents receiving growth hormone treatment. *Lancet* 2000;**355**:610–3.

456. Mehls O, Broyer M. Growth response to recombinant human growth hormone in short prepubertal children with chronic renal failure with or without dialysis. The European/ Australian Study Group. *Acta Paediatr Suppl* 1994;**399**:8–7.

457. Watkins SL. Is severe renal osteodystrophy a contraindication for recombinant human growth hormone treatment? *Pediatr Nephrol* 1996;**10**: 351–4.

458. Boechat M, Winters W, Hogg R, Fine RN, Watkins S. Avascular necrosis of the femoral head in children with chronic renal disease. *Radiology* 2001;**218**:411–3.

459. Kaufman D. Growth hormone and renal osteodystrophy: a case report. *Pediatr Nephrol* 1998;**12**:157–9.

460. Picca S, Cappa M, Rizzoni G. Hyperparathyroidism during growth hormone treatment: a role for puberty? *Pediatr Nephrol* 2000;**14**:56–8.

461. Mehls O, Salusky IB. Recent advances and controversies in childhood renal osteodystrophy. *Pediatr Nephrol* 1987;**1**:212–23.

462. Haffner D, Zacharewicz S, Mehls O, Heinrich U, Ritz E. The acute effect of growth hormone on GFR is obliterated in chronic renal failure. *Clin Nephrol* 1989;**32**:266–9.

463. Tönshoff B, Tönshoff C, Mehls O, Pinkowski J, Blum W, F, Heinrich U, et al. Growth hormone treatment over one year in children with preterminal chronic renal failure: no adverse effect on glomerular filtration rate. *Eur J Pediatr* 1992;**151**:601–7.

464. Auernhammer CJ, Strasburger CJ. Effects of growth hormone and insulin-like growth factor I on the immune system. *Eur J Endocrinol* 1995;**133**:635–45.

465. Mentser M, Breen TJ, Sullivan EK, Fine RN. Growth-hormone treatment of renal transplant recipients: the National Cooperative Growth Study experience – a report of the National Cooperative Growth Study and the North American Pediatric Renal Transplant Cooperative Study. *J Pediatr* 1997;**131**:20–4.

466. Maxwell H, Rees L, for the British Association for Paediatric Nephrology. Randomised controlled trial of recombinant human growth hormone in prepubertal and pubertal renal transplant recipients. *Arch Dis Child* 1998;**79**:481–7.

467. Broyer M. Results and side-effects of treating children with growth hormone after kidney transplantation – a preliminary report. Pharmacia & Upjohn Study Group. *Acta Paediatr Suppl* 1996;**417**:76–9.

468. Stahnke N, Zeisel HJ. Growth hormone therapy and leukaemia. *Eur J Pediatr* 1989;**148**:591–6.

469. Nishi Y, Tanaka T, Fujieda K, Igarashi Y, Hirano T, Yokoya S, *et al.* Recent status in the occurrence of leukemia in growth hormone-treated patients in Japan. GH treatment study committee of the foundation for growth science, Japan. *J Clin Endocrinol Metab* 1999;**84**:1961–5.

470. Maneatis T, Baptista J, Connelly K, Blethen S. Growth hormone safety update from the national cooperative growth study. *J Pediatr Endocrinol Metab* 2000;**13**:1035–44.

471. Cochat P, Six-Beneton A. Adverse effects of recombinant human growth hormone in renal patients. *Proceedings of the Third Novo Nordisk Workshop on CRI* 1997:19–23.

472. Tyden G, Wernersson A, Sandberg J, Berg U. Development of renal cell carcinoma in living donor kidney grafts. *Transplantation* 2000; **70**:1650–6.

473. Mehls O, Wilton P, Lilien M, Berg U, Broyer M, Rizzioni G, *et al.* Does growth hormone treatment affect the risk of posttransplant renal cancer? *Pediatr Nephrol* 2002;**17**:984–9.

474. Malozowski S, Tanner LA, Wysowski D, Fleming GA. Growth hormone, insulin-like growth factor I and benign intracranial hypertension. *N Engl J Med* 1993;**329**:665–6.

475. Koller EA, Stadel BV, Malozowski SN. Papilledema in 15 renally compromised patients treated with growth hormone. *Pediatr Nephrol* 1997;**11**:451–4.

Subject index